youth helping youth: a Handbook

for Training Peer Facilitators

by
Robert D Myrick
and Tom Erney

Copyright ©1979, ©1985

Educational Media Corporation®
Box 21311
Minneapolis, Minnesota 55421

(under special arrangement with the authors)

Library of Congress Catalog Card No. 78-70544

ISBN 0-932796-02-8

Production editor—

Don L. Sorenson

Graphic design—

Earl Sorenson

Illustrations—

James S. Noreen

Printing (Last Digit)

10 9

DEDICATION

PHYLLIS EDWARDS-ERNEY
and
WAYNE J. MYRICK
Two caring and gentle facilitators

PREFACE

The theory, concepts, activities and practical suggestions found in this book are based upon the authors' experiences with peer facilitator programs throughout the nation and, specifically, the Buchholz High School program in Gainesville, Florida. This book and its companion book, *Caring and Sharing: Becoming a Peer Facilitator,* offer a plan of action for organizing and implementing a successful facilitator program. In particular, it is suggested that students can be trained in an academic class and that they can work with students in the schools at all levels. In addition, they can be facilitators of young people and adults in various community settings.

There are many people who have assisted us in our efforts. It is not possible to recognize everyone who has contributed to the culmination of this project. However, we want to recognize those who have been especially helpful.

Several professional educators and writers have stimulated our thinking and many have reacted to our ideas, including: Dr. Sidney B. Simon, Dr. Joe Wittmer, Dr. Ardyth Norem-Hebeisen, Dr. Verne Faust, Dr. Jim Gumaer, Dr. Barbara Varenhorst and Don Samuels.

There were many who participated in the early development of the peer program in Gainesville, while others exchanged ideas with us and participated in its growth: Dr. Dick Pyle, Dr. Jack Christian, Dr. James Longstreth, Dr. Boyd Ayers, Ann Henderson, Bob Schenck, Gayle Vel Dink, Jo Ann Jenkins, Jeff Whittle, John Evans, Mark Myrick, Ret Thomas and the students, parents and faculty of Buchholz High School.

Appreciation is also expressed to Dr. Ron Anderson, Dr. Nancy Mitchum, Dr. Bob Bleck, Beth Dovell, Sylvia Stuart, Jacque Sheppard, James Campbell, Dale Hurd, Marty Criss and Mercedes Busk— school counselors and teachers—who believed in the concept and who helped us develop ideas about field experiences.

In addition, school administrators—Christine Clark and Sue Griffith (Littlewood Elementary School), Joe Hudson (Myra Terwilliger Elementary School), Orus Kinney (Stephen Foster Elementary School), Bill Cake (Fort Clarke Middle School), Lonnie Bryant (Westwood Middle School)—and their faculties cooperated with us and were willing to try new ideas to enhance the learning and personal growth of their students.

A special tribute is given to Cindy Cumming, Belinda Hedick and Phyllis Erney who typed parts of the manuscript. Dr. Don Sorenson and Earl Sorenson provided technical assistance, suggestions and copy editing. Their help has been most valuable.

Finally, we wish to thank Phyllis Erney and Linda Moni, two very special people, who reacted to our ideas, listened to our concerns, shared in our enthusiasm and provided us with some timely support and encouragement.

RDM

TE

TABLE OF CONTENTS

PREFACE   iv

INTRODUCTION   1
Chapter I: PEERS AS HELPERS   7

Chapter Highlights   7
Guidlines for Training   8

Activities
1.1 Problems of Youth   10
1.2 Notes to Myself   12
1.3 What's Happening with Today's Youth?   13
1.4 Who Am I?   14
1.5 Who Are the Helpers?   16
1.6 One-way Communication   18

Chapter II: HUMAN BEHAVIOR AND   21
            INTERPERSONAL RELATIONSHIPS

Chapter Highlights   21
Guidlines for Training   22

Activities
2.1 Unfinished Sentences   25
2.2 Fifteen Things I Love to Do   26
2.3 I am Loveable and Capable-IALAC   27
2.4 Trust Circles, Walks and Cradles   29
2.5 Think of a Secret   31

Chapter III: ATTENTIVE LISTENING   33

Chapter Highlights   33
Guidlines for Training   34

Activities
3.1 Twenty Questions   37
3.2 Rogerian Listening   38
3.3 How I See the World   39
3.4 Role Reversal   41
3.5 The Gibberish Game   42

Chaper IV: THE FACILITATIVE RESPONSES   43

Chapter Highlights   43
Guidelines for Training   44

Activities
4.1 Learning to be Facilitative (Triads)   46
4.2 Let Me Help   47
4.3 The Opposite Sex   49
4.4 The Turning of the Question   51
4.5 Say Something Helpful   52

Chapter V: FACILITATIVE FEEDBACK: PRAISING   **57**
    AND CONFRONTING

Chapter Highlights   57
Guidelines for Training   58

Activities
    5.1 Positive Feedback (Go-around)   60
    5.2 The Absent Person   62
    5.3 Using Feedback with Others   64
    5.4 Strength Bombardment   66
    5.5 Amnesia Game   68

Chapter VI: RESPONSIBLE DECISION-MAKING   **69**

Chapter Highlights   69
Guidelines for Training   70

Activities
    6.1 Setting Priorities   72
    6.2 Good Decisions—Poor Decisions   74
    6.3 Western Union   76
    6.4 The Volunteer Experience   77
    6.5 Personal Contract   79

Chapter VII: ASSESSING SELF AND OTHERS   **81**

Chapter Highlights   81
Guidelines for Training   82

Activities
    7.1 Self-evaluation   84
    7.2 What Makes Success?   86
    7.3 Planning a Case Study   88
    7.4 People Scavenger Hunt   89
    7.5 How Do I Respond?   91

Chapter VIII: GETTING READY TO HELP OTHERS   **93**

Chapter Highlights   93
Guidelines for Training   94

Activities
    8.1 Preparing for Your First Assignment   95
    8.2 Getting Ready   96
    8.3 Accountability Log   98
    8.4 First Impressions   99
    8.5 The Application   101

Chapter IX: PROBLEM MOMENTS   **103**

Chapter Highlights   103
Guidelines for Training   103

Activities
    9.1 How I Handle My Problems   105
    9.2 What Should be Done Now?   106
    9.3 Role Playing   107
    9.4 Dear Abby   109
    9.5 In Times of Stress   111

Chapter X: GETTING ORGANIZED   **113**

Organizing Peer Facilitator Programs   113
Building a Support Base   116

Chapter XI: HERE'S WHAT YOU NEED—A CHECKLIST   **123**

Meeting Place   123
Meeting Times   125
Selection Process   125
Parents' Night   132
Parent Permission   134
Program Calendar   135
Curriculum Calendar   139
Code of Ethics   140
Etc., Etc., Etc. . . .   140

Chapter XII: FIELD EXPERIENCES FOR PEER FACILITATORS   **141**

Moving Into the Field   141
Laying the Groundwork   142
Working in the Schools   144
Working in Community Agencies   152
Preparing the Students   154

Chapter XIII: ACCOUNTABILITY: TELLING AND SELLING OTHERS   **159**

Being Accountable   159
Assessing Your Program   160
Promoting Your Program   177

Chapter XIV: THE NEW HELPERS: A REVOLUTION IN SCHOOL GUIDANCE   **179**

The Paraprofessional Movement   179
The Peer Facilitator Movement   184

Chapter XV: THE TRAINER AS FACILITATOR AND LEARNER   **197**

A Successful Peer Facilitator Trainer Is . . .   198
What Beginning Trainers Have Said   201
In Conclusion . . .   202

SELECTED REFERENCES FOR TRAINERS   **203**

BIBLIOGRAPHY   **204**

LIST OF TABLES

Table I	Continuum of Facilitative Responses	44
Table II	Responses by Elementary Students to the PFEI	167
Table III	Responses by Secondary School Students to the PFEI	169
Table IV	Responses by Middle School Students to the GEF	172
Table V	Responses by High School Students to the GEF	173

INTRODUCTION

Youth helping youth is one of the most important educational concepts that has received special attention within the last few years. Many young people are now being trained to help others. They are learnig to be effective listeners, group leaders and role models for each other. As students learn to facilitate the personal growth and development of themselves and others, educational programs become more effective and learning is enhanced.

Very few students can learn to "counsel" other students. Counseling is a special skill that takes extensive training, study and practice. However, all students can learn to "facilitate" other students. Some will be more effective than others, especially those who have received training in communication skills and interpersonal relationships, and who are participating in a "peer facilitator program."

Many counselors, teachers and administrators have expressed an interest in learning more about peer facilitator programs. These programs help extend guidance services at a time when there are increasing demands and needs by young people. Hundreds of students, who would not usually receive needed guidance and counseling because of limited resources, can be reached by putting to good use the most abundant source of assistance and influence on any school campus—its student body.

There are many types of peer faciltator programs. Some have developed with little planning, but have been relatively successful because of the caring, commitment and energy that characterizes the people involved. Still others have been even more successful because, in addition, they have developed well-organized and systematic training programs that involve special projects, field experiences and on-going supervision. This more systematic approach is what has captured the imagination of most educators and has increased their interest. It is this approach that is most appealing and is the wave of the future in education.

This book was written to help you develop a peer facilitator program. It is a trainer's manual—a handbook for the training of peer facilitators. In addition to suggesting ways that *Caring and Sharing: Becoming a Peer Facilitator* might be used as a student book, this manual describes how you can start a program in your school or augment the one that you already have.

Caring and Sharing: Becoming a Peer Facilitator is the companion book to this handbook. It contains nine chapters. Each chapter focuses on an important concept related to being a successful peer facilitator:

Chapter	Title
I	Peers as Helpers
II	Human Behavior and Interpersonal Relationships
III	Attentive Listening
IV	The Facilitative Responses
V	Facilitative Feedback: Praising and Confronting
VI	Responsible Decision-Making
VII	Assessing Self and Others
VIII	Getting Ready to Help Others
IX	Problem Moments

Students are encouraged to read each chapter and to use the three activities at the end of each chapter to help them learn more about the concepts. Some of these same activities can eventually be used in their work with others. As a peer facilitator trainer, you will want to read *Caring and Sharing: Becoming a Peer Facilitator* and become familiar with its concepts.

THE ORGANIZATION OF THIS BOOK

Chapters I-IX

The first nine chapters in this book parallel those in the student book. Rather than repeat the context of each chapter, *Chapter Highlights* are summarized for your convenience. Then, *Guidelines for Training* are presented. This particular section in a chapter consists of practical suggestions and ideas to consider as you help students explore the concept or skill being studied. It provides you with some additional rationale and explanation.

Finally, there are the *Activities*—five or more activities for each chapter. The first three or four are the same as those that appear in the student book. The last two are additional activities that could be used to supplement the others. You may select any of the activities for your students to experience, depending upon your own interest, skill, time and the nature of your program. You will note that this book also contains helpful hints for the trainer and discussion questions with most of the activities.

Chapters X-XV

Beginning with Chapter X, attention is given to helping you get organized and build a support base. Three different options for a peer facilitator program are discussed. The first two options (Peer Facilitator Clubs and Peer Facilitator Aides) are usually more limited in scope and training. If you choose one of these two options for your program, you will need to be more selective in the use of the material presented. This book was particularly designed to help you develop a Peer Facilitator Class, where a more extensive curriculum is required.

In Chapter XI a checklist is offered. It is, perhaps, the beginning of your own checklist and it will help you think about some important items that need early attention: meeting place, screening process, peer selection, working with parents and a program calendar. With a program calendar, you get a better perspective of your total program and the direction you are going. It is helpful to think of your program in phases and you will want to study this section carefully. The curriculum calendar is also on the checklist. After you have a picture of what your program is about and where you are headed, then more attention can be directed to the training curriculum.

Field experiences are the heart of a peer facilitator program. This term is used to refer to a setting in which students work or a project in which they are participating. There are many settings in which they might work. In Chapter XII some practical suggestions are given which will help you lay the groundwork.

One neglected aspect of peer facilitator programs in most schools is evaluation. It is important to tell others about your program. At times you will need to "sell" your ideas to others. It is helpful if you have some supporting data. Assessing your work and helping students assess their own is part of being accountable to yourself and others. When little impact is being made, adjustments can take place. When there is evidence of success, it is more personally rewarding.

Chapter XIII outlines some ideas that can help you be more accountable and provides some examples of assessment measures. These instruments are designed to help you and your students look at both "process" and "outcomes." In addition, some studies in which these instruments were used are presented briefly. They illustrate how data might be used in public relations.

Chapter XIV will increase your understanding of the events that have led to the development of peer facilitator programs in the United States. First, we examine the influence of the paraprofessional movement and related issues. Then, drawing upon the professional literature, the peer facilitator movement is reviewed. The section "Students as Peer Counselors and Peer Facilitators" will help you build a case for having a program in your school. It outlines some reasons why such programs and "new helpers" have come into existence. Some research findings are reported. For those who desire additional background and research, an extensive bibliography is presented at the end of the book. A selected set of references is also given.

The final chapter, Chapter XV, focuses on the trainer as facilitator and learner. There can be little doubt that trainers or directors of peer facilitator programs set the stage for what will happen. As a trainer, you are responsible for structuring the program, selecting the training activities and developing projects or field experiences.

The program can be as limited or as extensive as you want it to be. You play the most significant role in its development, its evolution and its future. What personal characteristics will you need to have? To develop? What is your role as a "facilitator of the facilitators?" Most important, what can you expect to gain from the time and energy you must give? You will not only be a trainer and facilitator, but also a learner. This can be the most exciting and rewarding part of your work.

HOW THIS BOOK CAN BE USED

The first nine chapters of this book, along with *Caring and Sharing*, provide a curriculum for training middle or high school peer facilitators. The other six chapters describe practical suggestions for organizing a program in a school. However, with some adaptations, this book can help trainers develop peer facilitator programs in a variety of settings.

The basic principles and communication skills underlying the training of peer facilitators are relevant to all age levels. These same concepts apply to training facilitators in college and university settings, such as dormitories and learning centers. They have meaning for the training of adult volunteers who work in school and community settings. Also, sponsors of various youth groups, such as Girl/Boy Scouts, YMCA, YWCA, 4-H Clubs and other organizations, will find this book helpful. Paraprofessionals in a variety of settings, such as nurses' aides and workers with disadvantaged youth, will also benefit from knowing more about facilitating others.

People need people. There will never be enough counselors and therapists to serve those who need help. We need more "helpers." A preventive approach is also called for—one that helps people learn more about themselves and how to facilitate the personal growth of others. As a trainer of peer facilitators, you will play a significant role in making our schools, community and society more responsive and better places to be. We hope that this book will prove helpful in your efforts.

peers as helpers

CHAPTER HIGHLIGHTS

(Caring and Sharing, pages 1-14)

This beginning chapter discusses the need for young people to "get involved" by reaching out and caring about the lives of others. Some statistics are presented which help illustrate the intensity of the conflict and confusion that is being experienced by many young people today. The point is made that the relatively calm, dependable and predictable society of the past has been replaced by a frantic, quick-changing and unpredictable present.

Two case studies are presented which further illustrate problems confronting youth. This is followed by a definition of the term "peer facilitator," which has been deliberately chosen to replace the term "peer counselor." It is a term that will be used throughout the book. The chapter concludes with a brief outline of the ideas to be introduced in the following chapters.

GUIDELINES FOR TRAINING

I. This is one of the most exciting times to be involved as a trainer of peer facilitators. The enthusiasm and energy of being involved in something innovative and "special" generally helps create an atmosphere in which you can do some of your most meaningful and intense teaching. It is important that you, too, show your excitement and personal involvement. The behaviors that you model during the first few weeks will help set the tone for what is to follow.

Developing a comfortable, accepting and relatively free environment is perhaps the primary objective for the first few weeks. Very little will be accomplished until there is a genuine group cohesiveness and a rapport between students that allows them to trust each other. Through the strategies and activities outlined in the book, students can learn to develop mutual trust and to foster an accepting atmosphere.

This kind of environment will make it much easier to discuss ideas and to explore cognitive concepts later. Lectures and other trainer presentations should probably be kept to a minimum at this point. *Students learn best by doing.*

II. One effective way to help bring about a caring and sharing atmosphere in the class is to set aside a certain amount of time called "Comfort and Caring." This is a special time during the day, usually at the first part of the class, when students have an opportunity to make statements about experiences in their lives. There is no attempt to encourage interaction or exploration in any detail; rather, it is a time for students to *listen to each other and to become more aware of what others are experiencing.*

As a trainer, you may find that some of your facilitators are unaware of the many problems confronting some of today's youth. In addition, some of them are more aware of certain kinds of problems than they are of others. While any problem may seem rather minor to an "outsider," it is important for the facilitators to begin developing empathy or understanding for the feelings and situations others encounter.

More often than not, however, "Comfort and Caring" moments focus on the positive events in the students' lives. It is important that they have an opportunity to talk about rewarding and exciting times in their lives. As students share their ideas and listen to one another, they discover more about themselves and others. This special time also contributes to the building of group cohesiveness and encourages students to be more open with each other.

III. The presentation of data and statistics, the showing of films, the reporting of newspaper and magazine articles and presentations by outside speakers can add to the material presented in the book. In addition, when local statistics are available, this heightens the interest of the facilitators and increases their awareness of problems.

IV. It is important to explain the purposes and objectives of your program, especially in the first week. As soon as the facilitators have some understanding of why the program exists and what the program is attempting to do, they will have a better foundation upon which to develop their skills. They need, to some extent, a philosophical and theoretical rationale. Ideas and concepts will be more relevant and the techniques that they practice will be more meaningful if they have some idea as to the purpose of the program.

Most trainers of peer facilitators find it essential to explain their expectations early in the program. You may want to outline your expectations in a handout that would be distributed to the group. These can always be revised, but at least they have some idea of the direction in which you plan to move.

V. The term "peer facilitator" deserves special attention. This term is becoming more popular because it presents fewer problems to students who are systematically organized to help others. The term "peer counselor" has been used in the past, but this has presented more problems. Some parents, for example, have complained that they do not want their children being "counseled" by another student.

By substituting the word "facilitator," there seems to be less of a threat and there is more acceptance by parents. Moreover, the term "counseling" is a confusing one. It often implies deep secrets, privileged communication and expert advice. Since this is not the focus of a peer facilitator program, the term "counseling" is used sparingly. *Peer facilitators facilitate others to think about themselves.* They can help facilitate a class discussion or facilitate a group activity. In other words, the emphasis is upon using skills that promote more effective communication and personal exploration.

In addition, while the program could be perceived as a class in leadership, the term "peer facilitator" implies that the student is a helper and not a director. It suggests that students will do what they can to encourage and promote communication, rather than guide someone to a specified goal.

As facilitators become more effective, they enable others to do things that facilitate themselves toward a goal. Finally, the term "peer facilitator" seems to communicate more clearly the objectives of the program.

Activity 1.1:
PROBLEMS OF YOUTH
Caring and Sharing 11

PURPOSE:

To give consideration to major problems being experienced by young people today.

MATERIALS:

Pencil/pen.

PROCEDURE:

(1) Looking at the eight problem areas listed below, decide which problem you feel is the *main* concern of young people today. Mark a "1" in the blank next to the problem.

(2) Continue to rank order the rest of the problems until you have ranked *all* eight.

(3) Pair up with another person and compare your rankings. Be sure to listen carefully to the explanations your partner gives for their rankings.

EIGHT PROBLEMS CONFRONTING YOUTH TODAY

_____ Achieving in School
_____ Getting Along with Parents
_____ Changing Sexual Attitudes in Society
_____ Feelings of Loneliness
_____ Use of Illegal Drugs
_____ Abuse of Alcohol
_____ Making a Career Choice
_____ Making Friends

HELPFUL HINTS:

You may want to add additional problems to the eight listed above. Be sure to stress the importance of listening to your partner rather than debating.

DISCUSSION:

(1) Explain the reasoning for choosing your top three problems. What causes you to see them as so important?

(2) What possible solutions do you see for any of the problems mentioned?

(3) If you were a parent of a teenager, would your rank order change?

(4) How would you attempt to help a friend who was experiencing one of these problems?

NOTES TO MYSELF
Caring and Sharing   12

PURPOSE:

To encourage the students to take notes and keep a record of the activities they experience. To assist them in learning more about themselves.

MATERIALS:

A spiral notebook or stenographer's pad; pencil/pen.

PROCEDURE:

(1) Put your name on the front cover. You may also want to put a design or picture on the front that symbolizes something important to you.

(2) Take notes on the activities you do in class. Especially write down any tips on how to use the ideas (e.g. activities) with others.

(3) Take notes on the presentations and concepts discussed.

(4) If you desire, you can also write down any thoughts, experiences or questions which are important to you.

HELPFUL HINTS:

You may want to have a special place in the room where the students can leave their notebooks at the end of each class. This will insure that they have them the next day. Let them "personalize" their books with drawings and sayings. Emphasize that these books are personal, confidential and not to be read by others without permission. If this occurs, use the situation to discuss the issues of trust, privacy and confidentiality and the "urges" some have to violate these rights.

DISCUSSION:

None.

WHAT'S HAPPENING WITH TODAY'S YOUTH?

Caring and Sharing   13

PURPOSE:

To help sensitize the class to problems facing today's youth.

MATERIALS:

Any publication—newspapers, journals, magazines and so forth.

PROCEDURE:

(1) Find an article written in a newspaper or magazine (or any other media) that describes a problem that is confronting today's youth.

(2) Bring it, or a copy, to class.

(3) With another member of the class or a group, complete the statement:

"There is a need for young people today to. . . ."

(4) Put your material on a bulletin board or reference shelf for the rest of the class to see and use.

HELPFUL HINTS:

In addition to those listed in the student book, a bulletin board may be helpful to display the most interesting material. Perhaps a reference corner or table would be useful. In some instances art work can be used—posters—to dramatize the need for more peer helpers.

DISCUSSION:

(1) Who is responsible for the problems facing today's youth?

(2) When young persons experience problems, where can they turn for help? Who are the helpers?

(3) What problems do you see as the most critical facing students in this school? What problems are the same for adults? What are some examples of problems that are not shared by all?

WHO AM I?
Caring and Sharing 14

PURPOSE:

To stimulate student thought as to their personal development. To provide a vehicle for the trainer to get to know each student better.

MATERIALS:

Paper and pencil/pen.

PROCEDURE:

(1) Write an introductory paragraph to your *Who Am I* paper which presents most of your "vital statistics" (i.e. birthdate, birthplace, people with whom you currently live, their occupations and so forth). Include any other factual information which seems important.

(2) Focus the rest of your paper on the following issues:

    A. What you enjoy doing—hobbies, athletics and so forth.

    B. Significant events in your life.

    C. Major beliefs and values you hold and how you came to hold these beliefs/values.

    D. Questions/concerns you have about life.

    E. Your plans for the future.

You may put these issues in any order you choose.

(3) Be sure to proofread your paper to insure that it is an accurate representaton of who you are.

HELPFUL HINTS:

These papers are often very personal and they sometimes generate a great deal of emotional introspection. "Grading" these papers in a traditional way can inhibit a student's honest sharing and may result in a superficial response to the assignment. A more productive approach is to respond to certain statements with clarifying/challenging questions and/or comments which encourage students to think more about their statements. Your responses might become more of a "dialogue" between you and the student.

DISCUSSION:

(1) What feelings did you have as you were writing your paper?

(2) Summarize who you are in ten words or less.

(3) Examine your choice of words. Why did you use certain words to describe yourself and not others?

(4) If this paper were written by your father, what would be different? The same? What if it were written by your mother?

(5) What makes it so difficult for most people to describe themselves?

Activity 1.5:
WHO ARE THE HELPERS?

PURPOSE:

To learn more about people who are in the helping professions and the nature of their work.

MATERIALS:

An interview sheet or checklist, which may or may not be designed prior to the interview.

PROCEDURE:

(1) Have the students make a list of occupations or jobs in the local area that involve helping other people.

(2) After the list is completed, have them think of people that they know who provide such helping services to others.

(3) Have each student identify persons that they can interview regarding their work.

(4) Each student then interviews a helping person, using a checklist as a guide.

(5) Have the students write a report on their experience and summarize their findings.

HELPFUL HINTS:

This experience can be more meaningful if the class decides upon some common questions that they would like to ask all of the people in the helping professions. Let the class, as a group, decide upon the questions that all might use, although other questions might be asked too. Here are some examples:

(a) What do you like best about your work? Least?

(b) What's an example of a difficult situation where you feel tense when working with someone?

(c) What skills do you think are absolutely necessary for a helping person?

(d) What kind of people do you think are most effective in your work? What are their characteristics?

DISCUSSION:

(1) Lead the class in a discussion of their feelings, drawing upon such leads as those listed above.

(2) What are the common themes, characteristics, findings, and so forth that seem to go through the reports?

Activity 1.6:
ONE-WAY COMMUNICATION

PURPOSE:

To learn about one-way and two-way communication systems.

MATERIALS:

(1) Each of the three figures shown in this activity should appear on separate sheets of paper.

(2) Each student will need a pencil and three pieces of paper.

PROCEDURE:

(1) This activity might be preceded by a discussion of one-way and two-way communications. Have the students identify some examples of one-way communication (e.g. teacher lectures, teacher talking with back to students, announcements over the public address system, student conduct books, posted rules and policies).

Two-way communication involves an *interaction* process in which both the receiver and the sender of information can ask for more information or for some clarification.

Figure 1.1

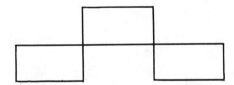

(2) Someone should volunteer to be the sender. Each student should have a piece of paper and a pencil and be prepared to follow the sender's directions. Hide the sender from view. The sender has three minutes to describe Figure 1.1, using any directions that seem to be helpful in an attempt to get the rest of the class to draw the figure on their papers.

Since this is to be one-way communication, the class is not to see Figure 1.1 or ask any questions from the sender. They simply follow the directions as the sender gives them.

Note: Confusion usually exists at this time and you may want to make notes of the group's reaction so that it can be discussed later. How did they behave in their confusion?

(3) When three minutes are up, ask each receiver to write one word that best describes what they are feeling at the moment about the experience.

(4) Let the sender show Figure 1.1 to the receivers and then lead a discussion with a focus on the feelings and behaviors. Unless the sender is an exception, very few students will have a accurate drawing. Other questions might be: How did the sender feel? How did the absence of gestures and eye contact make a difference?

Figure 1.2

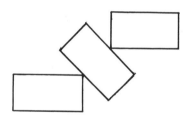

(5) *Begin a second round with a new sender* and use Figure 1.2. Repeat the procedures outlined above. However, this time the receivers, as a group, *may ask five questions* during this three minutes.

You will notice that this is a more difficult drawing, but with more two-way communication, more students should draw it with some accuracy.

Figure 1.3

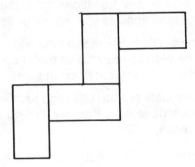

(6) *Begin the third round with a new sender* and use Figure 1.3. This time, however, do not hide the persons. The sender may use as much interaction as possible or needed with the receivers. Although still a more difficult drawing, there is usually more accuracy in the group.

In addition, take notice of senders' and receivers' feelings. It is possible that the sender with Figure 1.3 might be more frustrated because there is more demand by the receivers for interaction and information. Sender with Figure 1.1, for example, is simply giving information and may sense a feeling of control, calmness and security. Receivers generally feel more confident with Figures 1.2 and 1.3.

HELPFUL HINTS:

This activity might be enhanced by having the students experience one-way and two-way communications prior to the activity. Those experiences can then be reference points for discussion later.

DISCUSSION:

(1) Can you think of some examples where one-way communication led to some miscommunication or a loss of accuracy?

(2) How is the behavior of the receivers similar to other situations in life? The senders?

Chapter II

human behavior and interpersonal relationships

CHAPTER HIGHLIGHTS
(Caring and Sharing, pages 15-40)

An understanding of human behavior and the characteristics of the helping relationship is essential if peer facilitators are to have some degree of confidence in their work. Eight concepts of human behavior are outlined to help build a rationale for understanding others. These are:

1. We all have basic needs.

2. Everything we do is directed to some goal.

3. Our self-concept influences all our behavior.

4. Our self-concept is learned and can change.

5. Our self-concept is influenced by the consequences of what we do.

6. We are always learning and changing.

7. Increased self-awareness leads to responsible decision-making.

8. We learn from each other.

The characteristics of helping relationships, or the helping conditions, are also introduced. It is these characteristics upon which any peer facilitator program is founded. They are:

(1) *Listening attentively.*

(2) *Understanding the other person's point of view.*

(3) *Accepting the person.*

(4) *Caring enough to be committed and involved.*

(5) *Being genuine.*

The chapter concludes with an emphasis on the importance of developing interpersonal skills—especially those related to: (a) listening, (b) selectively responding, (c) giving feedback and (d) making decisions.

GUIDELINES FOR TRAINING

I. Most trainers who read this chapter will soon discover that not "everything" has been included. As in many books of this kind, there always seems to be something that is missing or that could be added. This is particularly true when it comes to outlining a theory of human behavior and the essential characteristics of a helping relationship. Every trainer will, no doubt, want to embellish the ideas presented in this chapter. These ideas are likely to come from one's own special interest or academic preparation.

No attempt is made to present a comprehensive theory of personality. While trainers are not discouraged from focusing on other concepts of human behavior that can be helpful to peer facilitators in their work, here are some words of caution: *Keep it simple!*

II. The eight principles for understanding human behavior were primarily drawn from the humanistic or "self" theorists. This theory is phenomenologically based and is not necessarily concerned with causation. Rather, it gives more attention to the individual as an experiencing organism and one who is influenced by affect (feelings) and present interactions.

Some fundamental constructs in this approach are *self-concept* and the *perceptual field*. Increased self-awareness is viewed as crucial to defining an individual's self-concept. The perceptual or phenomenal field is reality for the individual. Everything that a person does is designed to maintain or enhance the self-concept—to satisfy needs as the person experiences and perceives them. This theory has been the foundation for client-centered counseling, but the rationale for peer facilitating goes beyond this traditional approach.

Self-theorists have provided us with a relatively simple understanding of human behavior and one that peer facilitators can relate to. Such a theory emphasizes the importance of a cooperative partnership as part of the helping process. It gives special attention to respect, acceptance and understanding. It lends itself to a focus upon techniques and strategies that elicit or create a helping relationship. In addition, it emphasizes that the helping person, in order to create helping conditions, must be able to be warm, genuine, open and manifest other personal qualities that are desirable in most helping relationships.

Since this theory does not emphasize testing, diagnosis or other procedures that often foster dependence—or put the facilitator in the role of an "expert"—it was selected as the most practical and feasible theory to draw upon. This is not to ignore the importance of other theories and other specific techniques. As peers become more effective and efficient in their work, the trainer may want to add additional concepts.

III. Likewise, the five helping characteristics discussed in this chapter were selected from many that have been described by scholars and researchers in the fields of guidance, counseling and therapy. In particular, it seemed that understanding, acceptance, caring, commitment and genuineness are terms that are easily understood and can provide a peer facilitator with a basic understanding of the helping relationship. Moreover, the characteristics of being a good listener and using appropriate interpersonal communication skills appear to complete the picture of an effective peer facilitator.

IV. The activity, (2.5) *Think of a Secret* (page 31 in this book), can help students learn directly about the helping characteristics. It draws upon their own experiences and makes the helping conditions more meaningful to them. No doubt there will be many more helping words suggested than the five characteristics emphasized in this chapter. These may be added, of course, but again the idea is to *keep matters simple*. If warmth, humor, sincerity, respect and so forth are words that have special meaning for a peer facilitator (or trainer), then they may very well be added to the five that are singled out in this chapter. A long list of helping characteristics, however, can confuse the issue. Students will be interested in knowing *what they must do* in order to be perceived as a helping person.

UNFINISHED SENTENCES

Caring and Sharing 37

PURPOSE:

To explore the concept of helping.

MATERIALS:

Pencil/pen.

PROCEDURE:

(1) Complete the following unfinished sentences:

    A. Helping is . . . .

    B. Caring is . . . .

    C. The most important quality of any good friend is. . . .

    D. If I had a problem, I would feel most comfortable talking with . . . (name) because. . . .

    E. Young people who become involved in illegal activities do so because. . . .

(2) In groups of four, share your responses to the unfinished sentences and explore your ideas and feelings.

HELPFUL HINTS:

Encourage the students to complete the sentences with the first words that come to their minds. Ask them not to spend a great deal of time contemplating their responses. This is a time for spontaneity. More concentrated thought can take place during the discussion.

DISCUSSION:

(1) Is it possible for a person to "not need others?"

(2) Is it really possible for one person to "help" another?

(3) What song/poem/quote best illustrates what "helping" means to you? (e.g., *Bridge Over Troubled Waters, You've Got A Friend*)

(4) What are some "problems and pitfalls" of being a helping person?

FIFTEEN THINGS I LOVE TO DO
Caring and Sharing 38

PURPOSE:

To consider what is prized and cherished about life. . . what sustains and energizes us.

MATERIALS: An 8½ x 11-inch sheet of paper; pencil/pen.

PROCEDURE:

(1) Draw a line down the middle of your paper.

(2) On the left side of the paper, list *Fifteen Things in Life That I Love to Do.*

(3) After completing your list, divide the right side of your sheet into five narrow columns.

(4) Now, code your list in the following manner:

A. Put a "$" sign beside any item which *costs* more than $5.00 each time you do it.

B. Put an "R" beside any item which involves *risk*. The risk may be emotional, spiritual or physical.

C. Put a "U" beside an item which you think others would think as *unconventional*.

D. Write an "F" next to any item which you think will *not* appear on your list in five years.

E. Put a ★ beside the *three most favorite* activities on your list.

(5) Get into groups of four and take two minutes each to talk about your list.

HELPFUL HINTS:

Some people start to struggle after listing 7-10 things. You may need to do a little "pump-priming" by having them consider what they love to do: indoors/outdoors. . .fall/winter/ spring/-summer. . . alone/ with people. . . and so on.

DISCUSSION:

(1) What did you learn about yourself by doing the codings?

(2) How similar would your parents' lists be to yours?

(3) What other codings can you think of?

(4) Were there any surprises after you studied your coding?

(5) What purpose do the codings serve in this activity?

Activity 2.3:

I AM LOVEABLE AND CAPABLE—IALAC
Caring and Sharing   39

PURPOSE:

To help students become more aware of the impact that their actions and words have on others.

MATERIALS:

The *IALAC* Story; paper; pencil/pen.

PROCEDURE:

(1) Read the *IALAC* Story. *(Caring and Sharing, pages 39-40)*

(2) Make a list in your *Notes to Myself* notebook of the people who have torn your *IALAC* sign during the past week. Be sure to note what behavior resulted in the tearing away.

(3) Now, make a list of the people whose *IALAC* sign you have torn in the past week. Also, record what behavior caused the tearing away.

(4) Finally, write five to eight suggestions you have on the following topic: "What Can be Done to Combat Sign-Tearing in our Society?"

(5) Share your suggestions with others in your class.

HELPFUL HINTS:

This story often has a profound effect upon students. They are able to identify some concrete behaviors that influence self-concept development and become more aware of how devastating "killer statements" and "put-downs" can be.

If you (or your students) are telling the *IALAC* story to others, you might wear an *IALAC* sign taped on your chest and tear the sign at the appropriate moments. The visual impact of seeing someone's self-esteem torn away is powerful.

You can refer back to this story at various times during the year. Remind your students that their verbal and non-verbal behaviors can make quite a difference in how others feel about themselves.

DISCUSSION:

(1) What happens when a person's sign begins to read: "I am *un*loveable and *in*capable."?

(2) Can you think of others who might feel this way about themselves?

(3) How is "joking around" and "kidding" different from putting someone else down?

(4) What are some positive ways to respond when someone tears your *IALAC* sign?

(5) Which is more harmful— persons having their signs torn down by others or persons who tear their own signs?

TRUST CIRCLES, WALKS AND CRADLES

PURPOSE:

To help students develop a sense of trust by experiencing some non-verbal exercises.

MATERIALS:

None.

PROCEDURE:

(A) Trust Circle

(1) Members form a close circle. A volunteer is passed around the circle by the shoulders and upper torso. This person stands in the center of the circle with eyes closed as the group moves the person around or across the circle. Members take turns being passed.

(2) *Discussion:* How did it feel to be passed around? How did it feel to help pass someone around? Were some people passed differently than others? Was your group playful or serious? Aggressive or gentle?

(B) Trust Cradle

(1) Members form two lines, one on each side of a volunteer who is lying on the floor. The group picks the person with someone supporting the head of the volunteer.

(2) The volunteer, with eyes closed, should relax as much as possible while the group rocks forwards and backwards. The person may be raised up and down, all with a rocking motion.

(3) *Discussion:* How did it feel to be cradled? What were some of your thoughts as you cradled different members of the group? Did you experience any hesitation or resistance? If so, when? Did it disappear or reduce?

(C) Trust Walk

(1) Members of the class are paired up, with one person designated as the guide and the other as the blind person. The blind person is led around the room (or throughout an area) by the guide.

(2) After ten minutes, reverse roles.

(3) *Discussion:*   How did it feel to be the guide? The blind person? What were some interesting blind experiences? What was the most difficult part of this experience? How did it affect the feelings you have for each other? What did you learn about the issue of trust from this experience?

(D) Trust Fall

(1) In this experience, one person stands with back to two others who act as "catchers." With arms extended sideways, the person falls backwards and is caught by the two catchers.

(2) *Discussion:* How did it feel to fall? Did you wonder if you would fall to the ground and not be "saved?" How did it feel to have the responsibility of "catching" another person? What risks were taken?

HELPFUL HINTS:

These activities are popular ones that have been around a long time and passed down from one group leader to another.   While they can help students become more involved with the issue of trust, the following should also be considered:

(1) Exclude people who have a history of back injuries. Other physical conditions might also exclude some individuals from participating.

(2) Because these activities involve physical touching and there is some physical risk, care should be taken to introduce the activities as an educational experience.

(3) Some members may not feel comfortable being touched by others, or some may fear injury. No group pressure should be put upon anyone who does not wish to volunteer.

(4) If you plan to use a large area and if you will have some problems supervising the activities (such as the trust walk), be sure to emphasize responsibility, as well as adventure and fun.

Activity 2.5:
THINK OF A SECRET

PURPOSE:

To help students become more sensitive to the characteristics of a helping relationship.

MATERIALS:

Small slips of paper, which can be used by students to record their words, pencil/pen.

PROCEDURE:

(1) Begin by saying: "I want you to think of a secret, something that you've never told anyone else before. Or, if you have, perhaps only to one other person. It can be a secret thought or it may be something that you have done. *By the way, you are not going to be asked to write down your secret or tell it to anyone.* Now take 30 seconds and think about that secret."

(2) Continue with: "Okay, stop. Look around the group (class) and decide what it would take from the group before you would be able to tell them about your secret. Now, write one word or phrase that tells what you need. Do that now!"

(3) Collect the slips of paper with the words or phrases. There is no need to identify the writers. Rather, summarize the words and phrases by writing them on the chalk board and tallying those that are the same. Record all the thoughts, even those that imply there is no way the secret could be shared.

(4) After all responses have been recorded, discuss the meaning of the words.

Option: Ask them to think of a favorite teacher and then of a teacher who was not a favorite. In this case the students write two words, underlining the one that describes the favorite teacher. Two lists are made and then compared.

HELPFUL HINTS:

This activity is designed to have the students experience the conditions of a helping relationship. They draw upon their own experiences, which seems to be more effective than memorizing a list of helping characteristics. The most common words tend to be: *trust, confidentiality, acceptance, understanding, a similar experience and caring.* In addition, other popular helping words can be added in the discussion or likened to the words that appear (e.g. *warmth, respect, personal regard, interest, good listener, non-judgmental, time, love* and so forth).

DISCUSSION:

(1) How are these words different from each other?

(2) How would you define them?

(3) Do you hear any themes? What are they?

(4) Notice that such words as *expert, knowledgeable, psychiatrist, experienced, certified counselor, college graduate, must be of the same race, sex or age* are usually absent. What implication does this have for being a peer facilitator?

(5) What about the words that suggested a person could never foresee a time when they could share their secret? What does this say about the group? About the person's outlook on people?

(6) Of what value is there in sharing a secret with someone?

(7) Are there secrets that should probably be kept to one's self, except under unusual circumstances?

(8) What determines how "serious" a person's problem or secret is?

(9) Why do some people feel that they must keep an experience secret from others, while others who have experienced a similar thing quickly disclose the matter when asked?

(10) Is a person who is always willing to tell private thoughts and experiences to others "more healthy and more together" than those who are more cautious?

Chapter III

attentive
listening

CHAPTER HIGHLIGHTS
(Caring and Sharing, pages 41-56)

The art of listening is explored in Chapter III. Listening seems like such an easy skill that many people overlook its significance and the impact that one person can have over another by being an attentive listener. Therefore, students are encouraged to analyze their own listening habits and to reflect upon the listening style of others around them.

The *art of listening* is presented in six parts:

(1) *Focus on the person who is talking.*

(2) *Be aware of the feelings of the talker.*

(3) *Differentiate between unpleasant and pleasant feelings.*

(4) *Show that you understand what is being said.*

(5) *Be a selective listener.*

(6) *Avoid labeling or judging the talker.*

A special emphasis is placed upon listening for *pleasant* and *unpleasant* feelings. A list of feeling words is provided to help build the facilitators' affective vocabulary and to assist them to become more aware of how feelings are related to behavior.

GUIDELINES FOR TRAINING

I. Attentive listening is critical in all phases of peer facilitating. Inexperienced facilitators will often focus on the first stated concern of the person with whom they are talking. In addition, there is a tendency for beginning facilitators to rush through the early moments of an interview, attempting to get to the issue or problem. Unfortunately, this is not conducive to developing a helping relationship. It emphasizes *solutions* more than the *process* of thinking, feeling and exploring. Therefore, special attention has been given to the experience of *listening*.

By using some activities that focus on "non-listening" as well as listening, the students will begin to identify in their personal lives those ideas that they have been reading about.   *The experiencing of the activities* is the key to teaching the six steps of attentive listening.

II. While many things might be said about listening, the point to be emphasized is that *feelings and behaviors are related and people cannot talk about ideas without expressing their feelings.* It is important for the trainer to demonstrate good listening habits. This might even be demonstrated before the class.   It could be illustrated by the type of dialogue between a trainer and a student. For example:

TRAINER: *"So, the other morning you were feeling depressed and lazy. When you are feeling that way, what do those feelings of depression and laziness make you want to do?"* (Feeling and Understanding/Questioning-Probing)

STUDENT: *"Well, I feel like just staying in bed and not coming to school."*

TRAINER: *"So, when you're feeling down and kind of out of it, you just want to stay home."* (Feeling and Understanding)

STUDENT: *"Right. But then I think about my grades and what my parents will say, so I usually get up and drag myself to school."*

TRAINER: *"In other words, you feel like staying at home but you usually come anyway."* (Clarifying)

STUDENT: *"Yeah. I come, but then my first period class is a bummer. It depresses me even more, so I just tune out everything else and daydream about what I'll do after school—and maybe over the weekend."*

TRAINER: *"It would be so much easier for you to stay at home, but you come to school anyway. Then when you get here, you spend a lot of your time daydreaming."* (Clarifying) *What kinds of feelings do you get when you daydream?* (Question)

STUDENT: *"I feel relaxed. I enjoy it a lot. Sometimes I worry about things, but most of the time it's pleasant. In fact, it's one of my favorite pastimes."*

TRAINER: *"It's pleasant and you enjoy it. It's tempting to daydream when things are not going well."* (Feeling and Understanding)

By illustrating the link between feelings and behaviors, you can help the facilitators to understand how these concepts are related and the importance of tuning into feelings behind the spoken words.

III. Special attention should be given to listening for *pleasant* and *unpleasant* feelings. Unless students are able to identify feelings as part of a conversation and categorize them into unpleasant or pleasant, then it will be almost impossible for them to grasp some of the communication skills that are to follow. Even if it takes additional time and more activities, this part of the training should not be passed over too quickly.

IV. Some additional attention may be given to differentiating between *accepting* and *condoning behavior.* Some students have difficulty learning that acceptance and agreement are not the same. A person can be *accepted* for being a human being and, at the same time, the person's behavior can be *discouraged* or even *confronted*. Perhaps the key to this subtle issue is the emphasis upon gaining more understanding of the person's point of view. With understanding comes *respect* and *acceptance.*

Discourage students from thinking: "Do I agree or disagree?" when listening to people talk about their ideas. Rather, it is more beneficial and facilitative to think: "I wonder how they feel?"; "How does a person have to feel in order to behave that way or say those kinds of things?"; "I wonder how this person came to hold that belief?"; or "Help me understand the reasons for your feeling and thinking as you do."

Thus, the emphasis is upon gaining a deeper and clearer understanding of the person, rather than evaluating and labeling that person.

TWENTY QUESTIONS
Caring and Sharing 54

PURPOSE:

To provide a structured means of getting to know another person. To practice asking and answering relevant questions.

MATERIALS:

None.

PROCEDURE:

(1) Pair up with another student—preferably someone with whom you seldom talk. Find a private place in the room.

(2) Take turns asking any two questions you choose. The questions may be general or personal.

The person being asked the question has the "right to pass" on any question. Continue taking turns (asking two questions, then answering two questions) until each has asked and answered ten questions.

(3) After all questions have been asked and answered, take one minute and summarize what you learned about your partner.

HELPFUL HINTS:

Have the students pair with someone that they seldom interact with. This is a time for getting to know people better. If necessary, you can arrange the pairs to promote more interaction.

Give everyone an opportunity to share. If used often, a time limit of 7-10 minutes can be set.

DISCUSSION:

(1) What are two or three interesting questions that your partner asked you?

(2) What are some of the differences between talking with a friend and talking with someone that you hardly know?

(3) Who are four people that you would really like to play *Twenty Questions* with? How did you choose these four people?

Activity 3.2:
ROGERIAN LISTENING
Caring and Sharing 55

PURPOSE:

To develop a greater awareness of how involved and important the art of listening really is.

MATERIALS:

None.

PROCEDURE:

(1) Put yourself into a group with two other persons. One person assumes the role of referee (monitor) while the other two people agree to be the talkers.

(2) Pick a topic of mutual interest on which the talkers have different points of view.

(3) The beginning talker has one minute in which to express views on a controversial topic. During this time, the referee and the other participant listen.

(4) Once the first talker stops, the second talker *must summarize the key statements made by the previous speaker* before offering a point of view. The role of the referee is to insure that *this accurate summarizing takes place before the second person continues.*

(5) The two talkers continue to exchange points of view (after summarizing the previous statements of the other) until they agree that each understands the viewpoint of the other.

(6) The referee now changes place with one of the talkers. A new topic is chosen and the process continues.

(7) Write a short summary in your *Notes to Myself* notebook concerning your reactions to this activity.

HELPFUL HINTS:

You may need to present a list of controversial topics from which the students can choose—abortion, capital punishment, voluntary army, cremation, interracial marriage, the importance of a college education, the Equal Rights Amendment, and so forth.

There will be occasions during the year when there will be differences of opinion among the students and/or you. When these times happen, demonstrate how effective and powerful the *Rogerian Listening* activity can be by using it to resolve these real situations.

DISCUSSION:

(1) Who are three people that you wish you could teach this activity to in order to help them become better listeners?

(2) What would happen if you and your parents would do this whenever you are in conflict?

(3) What makes listening to someone who disagrees with us difficult?

Activity 3.3:
HOW I SEE THE WORLD
Caring and Sharing 56

PURPOSE:

To practice listening for pleasant and unpleasant feelings.

MATERIALS:

A large piece of paper that can first be cut into a circle and then into parts; pencils, magic markers or crayons.

PROCEDURE:

(1) Form a group with three or four other members of the class.

(2) The large piece of paper represents the world. Cut the paper into parts. Each person is given a part of the "world."

(3) On your portion of "the world," draw some symbols or pictures that represent some of your thoughts about how you see the world today.

(4) After the group has recorded their thoughts, all of the individuals, in turn, tell the group the meaning of their pictures.

(5) While each person is talking, the other group members listen for feelings—unpleasant and pleasant.

(6) After each person has finished, the group tries to remember the feelings that were shared. A list of these feeling words is made.

(7) After everyone has had a turn, look at the total list of pleasant and unpleasant words. Discuss your reactions.

HELPFUL HINTS:

After the members of the group have shared their individual points of view, have the group "reconstruct" the world by taping their individual pieces back together. Have the members summarize how their group sees the world and then compare the summaries of each group.

DISCUSSION:

(1) How many different feeling words did your group have? Which feeling words are the most commonly used by young people?

(2) What events have played a major part in shaping how you see the world today?

(3) Were there more pleasant or unpleasant feeling words used in your group? The class?

Activity 3.4:
ROLE REVERSAL

PURPOSE:

To help students gain a more accurate understanding of "perceptions" and to help them see themselves as others see them.

MATERIALS:

None.

PROCEDURE:

(1) Form groups of three or four. One person volunteers to talk about three minutes on the subject: *Something I Believe is True About Life.*

(2) The others in the group listen. After three minutes of listening and facilitating the talker, one member takes the talker's place (takes the chair, assumes the same posture and so forth) and imitates the person by expressing the same ideas as they heard them express.

(3) Others in the group, including the talker, discuss how accurate the person's portrayal was. Comments are made on choice of words, tone of voice, body posture and other observations.

HELPFUL HINTS:

Role reversal is not role playing. Each person assuming the part of the other person is encouraged to be as much like that person as possible. The same ideas are expressed, with the same choice of words—as much as possible.

DISCUSSION:

(1) How accurate was the role reversal? What might have been added to make it more realistic? What should have been eliminated to make it more realistic?

(2) How did the person assuming the role feel afterwards? Do you have a better understanding after trying to assume the role, or is it about the same?

(3) Talkers, after watching the role reversal, do you think the person has an accurate understanding of what you were trying to communicate?

Activity 3.5:
THE GIBBERISH GAME

PURPOSE:

To gain an understanding of how voice inflections and gestures play an important role in communication.

MATERIALS:

None.

PROCEDURE:

(1) Divide the class into small groups, with three or more students to a group.

(2) Groups are instructed to converse by using "gibberish." Gibberish is the use of nonsense syllables and sounds.

(3) After a few minutes, each group is asked (a) to slowly and gradually begin to exclude one of the three people from the conversation without deciding ahead of time who will be excluded and (b) to be aware of how they feel in that position.

Option: Using "gibberish," experience the phenomenon of being labeled, judged or evaluated. Use the same nonsense word (e.g. "Iddydish") with different intonations (e.g. affection, anger, indifference, etc.)—"You Iddydish!"

HELPFUL HINTS:

This can be a fun experience. It emphasizes the importance of "extra-verbal communication." It illustrates the importance of tone of voice, emotional intent with words and so forth.

DISCUSSION:

(1) How did it feel to be excluded? Included? How could you tell it was happening?

(2) Did the tone of your words, the intensity in expressing them, suggest your feelings? Your ideas?

(3) We cannot talk without expressing feelings. How is that illustrated in this activity?

Chapter IV

the facilitative responses

CHAPTER HIGHLIGHTS

(Caring and Sharing, pages 57-96)

Facilitating is viewed as both an *art* and a *science*. Most important, it is presented as a role with appropriate *skills that can be learned*. Attention is given to the importance of *knowing techniques, but as applied in the context of genuineness and sincere caring*.

Several hypothetical situations are presented and students are given the opportunity to make an initial response. A *Continuum of Facilitative Responses* is introduced, with special focus upon the following responses:

(1) *Advising and Evaluating*

(2) *Analyzing and Interpreting*

(3) *Reassuring and Supporting*

(4) *Questioning and Probing*

(5) *Clarifying and Summarizing Events*

(6) *Reflecting and Understanding Feelings*

These responses are rated respectively from low (1) to high (6). Students are encouraged to learn and practice the high facilitative responses (4, 5 and 6) and to increase the frequency of them in their work as peer facilitators. (See *Table II* in *Caring and Sharing* (Page 67) and *Table I* in *Youth Helping Youth* (Page 44).

Table I

CONTINUUM OF FACILITATIVE RESPONSES

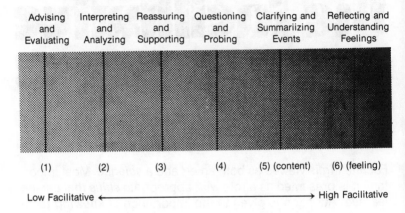

Advising and Evaluating	Interpreting and Analyzing	Reassuring and Supporting	Questioning and Probing	Clarifying and Summariizing Events	Reflecting and Understanding Feelings
(1)	(2)	(3)	(4)	(5) (content)	(6) (feeling)

Low Facilitative ← ⎯⎯⎯⎯⎯⎯⎯⎯⎯⎯⎯⎯⎯⎯⎯ → High Facilitative

GUIDELINES FOR TRAINING

I. Some responses seem to convey more understanding than others. In addition, some responses apparently increase the probability that the person who is responding will be perceived as a helping person—one who is understanding, caring, accepting and so forth. *Responding selectively* to what people say is one way in which a peer facilitator can become more effective.

II. While several response categories might have been presented, the *Continuum of Facilitative Responses* is used because it is simple to learn and students find it helpful to think:

"Increase the frequency of the high facilitative responses."

This phrase can be repeated over and over again, especially in the initial phase of training! Making high facilitative responses is incompatible to making low facilitative ones. Thus, students who increase the frequency of the high facilitative responses will elicit or create the helping conditions more than they would otherwise.

Also, the high facilitative responses enable students to engage individuals or groups in discussions and to facilitate talk without giving advice. Moreover, with such skills as high facilitative responses, the student need not be concerned about diagnosis or interpretation. However, it should be emphasized that *no response, by itself and out of context, can be rated as good or bad, correct or incorrect, helpful or not helpful.*

III. Perhaps the first step in learning to respond more selectively is identification and increased awareness of the various responses. Students can practice differentiating responses and selecting those that are rated as "most" facilitative. A second step might be for students to formulate their own responses, using them spontaneously in their work. As a general rule, the low facilitative responses are so common in our everyday language that it is not necessary to practice them, only to identify them and bring them to awareness.

Practice of the high facilitative responses is necessary because they are not common responses and because students will feel awkward and phony when they first use them. It should be remembered that *peer facilitators will use all of the responses.* They should. While we have learned a lot from the traditional client-centered counseling model, it is not necessarily the most effective role for peer facilitators to take. It is probably too far removed from the reality of peer interaction.

IV. This might also be a good time to give some attention to *nonverbal expressions* such as gestures, posture, tone of voice and so forth.

LEARNING TO BE FACILITATIVE (TRIADS)

Caring and Sharing 92

PURPOSE:

To give students an opportunity to practice using the facilitative responses.

MATERIALS:

The Facilitator's Report Card (Page 94 in *Caring and Sharing*); pencil/pen.

PROCEDURE:

(1) With two other people, form a group (triads). Number off: 1, 2 and 3. Let No. 1 be the talker, No. 2 the facilitator and No. 3 the observer.

(2) The talker begins by speaking to the facilitator for three minutes, while the observer watches and takes notes. The talker is to speak on "Something I Would Like to Change About Myself."

The facilitator assists the talker by responding with high facilitative responses—*reflecting feelings, clarifying ideas* and *asking open-ended questions*. Remember, no advice, no praise and *no interpretations*. Follow the lead of the talker.

The observer watches the facilitator and records observations by marking on the *Facilitator's Report Card.* After three minutes, the observer—using the report card—tells the facilitator what seemed to be happening (about two minutes is allowed for this part).

(3) Now, the same talker, facilitator and observer go through another three minute round. This time the talker speaks about "Something I Like About Myself," while the facilitator and observer repeat their same roles. Again, after three minutes, the observer gives a report.

(4) Switch roles in a second and third round (with the same talking assignments) until all three have been in each role.

(5) After each person has been in all three roles, discuss among yourselves: "How I Felt About Doing This Experience."

DISCUSSION QUESTIONS:

Here are some discussion questions and comments that might be helpful:

How is what you dislike (or like) about yourself related to your school life? Family life? Hopes for the future?

HELPFUL HINTS:

Have a chart posted on the wall (or drawn on the board) which indicates the three categories of high facilitative responses. Also, write an example of each type of response on this chart.

The role of the observer can be an uncomfortable one. Some peer facilitators will not like giving potentially negative feedback to any of their classmates. Urge the observer to be candid and helpful.

DISCUSSION:

(1) How do you feel when talking about yourself?

(2) Which part did you like best?

(3) Was it easier to talk about the negative or positive aspects of yourself?

(4) Which aspect was the easiest to facilitate?

(5) What did you learn from this experience?

Activity 4.2:
LET ME HELP
Caring and Sharing 95

PURPOSE:

To experience the effects of low and high facilitative responses when attempting to make a decision.

MATERIALS:

None.

PROCEDURE:

(1) Get a partner.

(2) Each of you think of your response to the following question: "What is one decision you are trying to make right now?" It may be a major or a minor decision. The only criterion is that it must be a real situation and your aren't sure what you should do.

(3) Decide who will be the talker and who will be the listener. The *talker* has two minutes to share the decision being contemplated. The *listener's* role is to use only the three *lowest* facilitative responses: advice, analysis and reassurance in attempting to assist the talker.

(4) After two minutes, reverse roles. The new listener once again uses only the *low* facilitative responses. Continue for two minutes.

(5) Each of you have had an opportunity to talk about your decision to a person using *low* facilitative responses. Now, take another two minutes to talk about your decision. This time the facilitator will use only *high* facilitative responses (open-ended questions, clarifying and summarizing and reflecting feelings).

(6) Share your reactions to this activity with the rest of the class.

HELPFUL HINTS:

You may want to do a quick demonstration of this activity before you have the students do it. Then, draw the *Continuum of Facilitative Responses* on the board and mark the six classifications. This will serve as a reference for any student who needs to recall the low and high facilitative responses.

DISCUSSION:

(1) What differences did you experience as a talker when they used the various responses?

(2) How difficult was it for your to keep from giving advice?

(3) What causes so many of us to want to be advice-givers and analyzers?

(4) What are your most common non-facilitative responses?

THE OPPOSITE SEX

Caring and Sharing 96

PURPOSE:

To practice listening, clarifying and responding to feelings. To learn about the thoughts and feelings of the opposite sex.

MATERIALS:

Chairs for an inner and outer circle arrangement.

PROCEDURE:

(1) Form two circles—one inside the other.

(2) All the boys sit in the inside circle while the girls occupy the outside chairs.

(3) As the girls listen (no comments), the boys talk about:

   A. What do you think it would be like to be a girl?

   B. What are the advantages?

   C. What are the disadvantages?

   D. The problems?

(4) After eight to ten minutes, from the girls' group should come:

   A. Four clarifying responses

   B. Four feeling responses

   C. Two questions

   D. One piece of advice or interpretation

The girls' responses should be related directly to what the boys have said.

(5) Now, change places—girls on the inside and the boys on the outside.

(6) Repeat the same procedures as above (3). This time the boys listen (without comment) while the girls discuss what it would be like to be a boy.

(7) The boys then respond as outlined in (4).

(8) Use the remainder of the time for open discussion.

HELPFUL HINTS:

This can be a very involved and emotional discussion. Oftentimes it is difficult for those in the outer circle to keep from reacting (verbally or non-verbally) to what is being said about them. Enforce the "no comments" rule. Otherwise, those in the inner circle may lose the flow of their thoughts and feelings. Also, interruptions are inhibiting.

Option: Another way of doing this activity is to have an empty chair in the inner circle. Persons from the "outer circle" can move in and have one minute to react to what is being said.

DISCUSSION:

(1) What confuses you about the opposite sex?

(2) How many of you know the meaning of the term "androgyny?" Are there any traits that are solely female? Male?

(3) How important is it for you to have a boyfriend/girlfriend? How do you come to feel as you do?

Activity 4.4:
THE TURNING OF THE QUESTION

PURPOSE:

To help students learn to reduce the amount of questions used in facilitating by turning them into statements (content or feeling focused).

MATERIALS:

Small slips of paper; pencil/pen.

PROCEDURE:

(1) Form the class into groups. Someone in the group volunteers to tell about something that has happened recently. After the person has made a brief statement, the group is asked to write a question—any kind of question—that they would like to ask.

(2) Members, in turn, read their own questions. Then say: "Behind each question is an assumption. See if you can eliminate the question by turning it into a statement. For some all you have to do is remove the question mark and read it as a statement (e.g. Were you tired? You were tired.). For others you will have to ask yourself what assumption was I making and then put it into words. Now, write that second response below your question."

(3) Have members read, first, their original questions, then, the changes they made or the statements.

(4) With the group, identify each statement as either a clarifying or summarizing statement (content focused) or a feeling and understanding statement (feeling word is present).

DISCUSSION:

(1) If it is so easy to turn questions into statements and thus make a higher facilitative response, why is it that facilitators are often accused of asking too many questions?

(2) How do you feel when a person just keeps asking questions?

Activity 4.5:
SAY SOMETHING HELPFUL

PURPOSE:

To help students learn to identify facilitative responses.

MATERIALS:

The Facilitator Response Inventory; pencil/pen.

PROCEDURE:

(1) Reproduce *The Facilitator Response Inventory* and distribute it to the students.

(2) Ask the students to follow the directions and check the items, indicating the type of response and their preference for responses (a forced choice).

(3) Divide the class into small groups, or perhaps put students in pairs and have them discuss their choices.

HELPFUL HINTS:

This activity is designed to help students learn to identify responses based on the six responses presented in the chapter. High facilitative responses (4, 5 and 6) or questioning, clarifying and understanding of feeling are suggested as best choices.

However, some students may argue in favor of other responses. In this case, try to understand their point of view. Let them build a case for selecting the item. This activity is also excellent for helping students discuss the question: "What determines whether a response in a given situation is facilitative or not?" The usual answer is: "If it helps the person move toward some positive goal." Remind the students that no response, by itself, can be labeled good or bad, correct or incorrect.

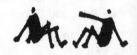

DISCUSSION:

(1) What responses did you prefer in the situations? Which choices were the most difficult to make?

(2) What is a facilitative response? How can one determine if a response is facilitative or not?

(3) Of what value is it to know how responses can be viewed as high or low facilitative?

(4) Can you think of two situations similar to those suggested by the items in the inventory and write some possible responses? Then, how would you identify them?

FACILITATOR RESPONSE INVENTORY

INSTRUCTIONS:

Listed below are some statements made by helpers and helpees (facilitators). Look at the helper statements and (1) decide which one you would prefer by checking it in the first column: (2) Then, identify what position (1-6, see page 44) that response might fall on the *Continuum of Facilitative Responses.* Indicate column.

(1) Helpee: "I know that I should talk with someone about my problem, but I'm not sure that I can."

Example:

<u>X</u> <u>4</u> **Helper Response A:**   "What keeps you from talking about it with someone?"

___ <u>3</u> **Helper Response B:**   "Well, everyone has problems. It's not so hard once you decide to talk about it."

(1) Helpee: "No matter how hard I study, my grades still aren't what they should be. It just isn't fair."

___ ___ **Helper Response A:**   "What kind of grades are you getting?"

___ ___ **Helper Response B:**   "It's frustrating to work at it like you do and not get better grades."

(Column labels at left:) Prefered Response / Response Position

(2) Helpee: "My boyfriend and I were getting along pretty well and then suddenly we started having these arguments about some of the weird things that go on at the parties we go to."

____ ____ **Helper Response A:** "You're not sure you like what's happening at the parties."

____ ____ **Helper Response B:** "Instead of arguing, you might talk with him about it at a time when you can both be rational and more objective."

(3) Helpee: "I'm feeling so much better now. I can see how some of the things I was doing just made me unhappy. Wow! What a difference!"

____ ____ **Helper Response A:** "You seem to be enjoying life more, now that you understand yourself a little better."

____ ____ **Helper Response B:** "I knew you would feel better after you got more understanding of the difficulties you were having. You're just too smart to have continued along the way you were."

(4) Helpee: "My dad thinks I should go in the service as soon as I graduate from high school. He keeps nagging me to talk to a recruiter and says that I can get an education in the Navy that would be better than any college. He won't even listen to my side."

____ ____ **Helper Response A:** "Because you're still dependent upon your parents, especially your dad, it's not easy for you to make up your own mind."

____ ____ **Helper Response B:** "Your dad has some strong opinions about what you might do after graduation and you are feeling some pressure to follow his suggestions."

(5) Helpee: "I don't see why I can't do it. All my friends are doing it."

____ ____ **Helper Response A:** "It's not good for you to be so influenced by what others do or say. You need to think about your future."

____ ____ **Helper Response B:** "You're thinking what's good for your friends is good enough for you."

(6) Helpee: "I get nervous when I'm giving a speech. I think I'd just as soon take a lower grade than get up and talk in front of an audience."

—— —— **Helper Response A:** "You're afraid to ge up in front of others because you think that they are evaluating you."

—— —— **Helper Response B:** "It makes you anxious to be in front of others."

(7) Helpee: "I've thought about the pros and cons and I still don't know what I should do. Tell me, what do you think I should do?"

—— —— **Helper Response A:** "I can't make a decision for you. You should depend upon your own judgment, not mine."

—— —— **Helper Response B:** "You seem uneasy about facing the consequences of making a decision."

(8) Helpee: " I've never tried to smoke pot, but some of my friends do. I know I'll probably give it a try sometime, just to see what it's like."

—— —— **Helper Response A:** "You think that you should try smoking pot because you have friends that do."

—— —— **Helper Response B:** "What are the consequences if you do or don't?"

(9) Helpee: "You know, the closer I get to graduation, the more confused I get about what I want to do."

—— —— **Helper Response A:** "What plans have you made so far?"

—— —— **Helper Response B:** "Time is running out and you might talk to a counselor about some opportunities. They have some good information in the guidance office."

(10) Helpee: "I find it very hard to express positive feelings to others, even those I love."

_____ _____ **Helper Response A:** "But, those kind of feelings are the ones that really count and make a difference in a person's life."

_____ _____ **Helper Response B:** "How do you think people might respond to you if you expressed your positive feelings?"

(11) Helpee: "I have a teacher who doesn't like me and there's no doubt that it's going to show in my grades."

_____ _____ **Helper Response A:** "Do you like the teacher?"

_____ _____ **Helper Response B:** "How do you feel about the teacher?

(12) Helpee: "You know, I haven't taken anything from a store for almost two months now. I'm just hoping that this shoplifting thing is over for good."

_____ _____ **Helper Response A:** "That's great! You've really made a lot of improvement."

_____ _____ **Helper Response B:** "That's great. But you're still not sure that you've got things under control."

(13) Helpee: "You probably think I'm phony. I can't seem to keep from lying about myself and others."

_____ _____ **Helper Response A:** "A lot of people feel phony at different times in their lives. We can't be perfect."

_____ _____ **Helper Response B:** "It's discouraging to be something less than what you want to be."

Chapter V

facilitative feedback : praising and confronting

CHAPTER HIGHLIGHTS

(Caring and Sharing, pages 97-128)

Feedback is an important skill in the communication process. Feedback is defined as "telling another person the kind of impact that person's behavior is having on you." It involves an honest reaction to another.

When giving feedback, the person tries to avoid giving advice, judging or labeling and focusing on things that can't be changed. A three-step feedback model is described:

(1) Be specific about the behavior.

(2) Tell how the person's behavior makes you feel.

(3) Tell what your feelings make you want to do.

Confrontation is viewed as a time when a person speaks about the unpleasant feelings being experienced. It is recommended that when people speak about *unpleasant experiences,* they also consider (a) having some "chips in the bank" (having tried to understand the other person's feelings and point of view); (b) having had a persistent unpleasant feeling; and (c) being selective in the choice of words—avoiding an intensity that would make the person defensive and turn away. Praise, on the other hand, is a time when the person speaks about *pleasant feelings* as related to someone's behavior.

Finally, the chapter concludes with a comparision of *direct* and *indirect* feedback. Direct feedback is a straightforward approach and directly follows the three-step feedback model. Indirect feedback also follows the three steps, but metaphors or descriptions of objects are used to describe the kind of impact that is experienced. The facilitative feedback model can be helpful in organizing one's thoughts and being systematic with praise or confrontation—either with an individual or a group.

GUIDELINES FOR TRAINING

I. In the early stages of training, "tuning into others" was emphasized. In this chapter students learn how to "tune into themselves" and to express their feelings, especially as related to another's behavior. The three-step feedback model provides the peer facilitator with a valuable tool and completes the set of responses needed to facilitate discussion with either an individual or a group. At first the model may seem a little awkward, but students are encouraged to practice it step by step. Such a model slows them down, helps them organize their thoughts and enables them to share their feelings in a more caring way.

II. After the students have practiced giving feedback in the order of the three steps, it is important to have them practice giving feedback by using a different order. For example, students might begin by speaking about their feelings first, then what those feelings make them want to do and, finally, concluding with the individual or group behavior that has contributed to those feelings. *Mixing the order, but always including the three steps, tends to provide versatility and reduces feelings of being stiff and phony.*

III. In general, it is a good idea to speak to all three steps in the facilitative feedback model. However, the first two steps have proven to be more critical and might be given the most attention.

IV. Some trainers of peer facilitators may object to the use of "makes me feel" and take the position that individuals are responsible for their own feelings. "No one can make a person feel anything." This position, of course, attacks the stimulus-response theory and argues that we are existential beings that are in control of ourselves—if we would only realize it.

We agree—at least in part. There is substantial evidence to suggest that, as human beings, we are conditioned to respond and to react in certain ways. Most important, our behavior is related to our feelings. Thus, the feedback model does not inhibit a trainer from emphasizing an existential or Gestalt approach.

In the early years of peer training, other expressions were used including the following: "When I am around you and you do (behavior), I experience (the feelings) and then I want to (behavior)." Thus, the words "it makes me" were eliminated. However, this phraseology is more sophisticated and, at times, too stiff for most students. Students did not identify with it as easily as with the model outlined in the chapter. The third step in the model emphasizes that the speaker is responsible for the behavior exhibited. Behavior does not necessarily mean that an automatic behavioral reaction is triggered, but it does stimulate feelings and these feelings do lead to behavior.

V. There may be other feedback models which can be helpful in the work of a peer facilitator, including National Training Laboratory models, "I-messages" and so forth. The model presented in this book has stood the test of time and the test of simplicity—as well as the test of effectiveness.

POSITIVE FEEDBACK (GO-AROUND)
Caring and Sharing   126

PURPOSE:

To help the students practice giving and receiving feedback and to help them learn more about themselves and others. This experience can also help build more group cohesiveness among the peer facilitators.

MATERIALS:

None.

PROCEDURE:

(1) Form a small group, about five people to a group. Get with people that you would like to talk with, telling them the impact they have on you and learning about the impact that you have on them.

(2) Review in your own mind, or perhaps in discussion with others, the three parts (steps) of giving feedback.

(3) Someone in the circle should volunteer to begin. The first volunteer then talks to each person in the group, in turn, giving each some positive feedback. The person receiving the feedback listens and makes no comments. *After the first volunteer has given each person in the group some feedback, another person then volunteers and gives feedback to each person.* Again, each member listens to the feedback and makes no comments. It can be helpful if you: a) call the person by name, b) look at them and c) talk directly to them.

(4) After the last person in the group has practiced giving feedback, have a group discussion about the experience. You may want to ask some questions or get some clarification about what was said.

HELPFUL HINTS:

Be sure to have the group in an open circle, in chairs or on the floor. Remove the desks or table barriers. Group members are not to interact during the feedback experience as this would prolong the activity and stimulate the group to become more involved than is necessary at this point. This is a practice session. But, because the feedback is real, it will have a significant impact on the group.

Option: This activity can also be done without the rule of "focus on the positive." As an open-ended experience, the person giving the feedback can speak to either pleasant or unpleasant feelings. In this case, caution the participants to remember the guidelines for giving such feedback.

Option: Same procedures, except use indirect feedback such as descriptions or metaphors (e.g. cars. flowers).

DISCUSSION:

(1) How did you feel when giving feedback to people in the group?

(2) Was it easier to give feedback to certain people than to others?

(3) Did you follow all three steps? What order did you use?

THE ABSENT PERSON
Caring and Sharing   127

PURPOSE:

To practice using the feedback model outlined in this chapter by focusing on someone outside the class.

MATERIALS:

An empty chair.

PROCEDURE:

(1) Form a circle with about five to six people. An empty chair is placed in the middle.

(2) Think of someone who is *not* sitting in the circle. As you think of that person, what is something that they do that you like? What kind of a pleasant feeling do you get? Then, when you have that feeling, what do you want to do?

(3) Now, imagine that the person is sitting in the empty chair. Tell that person your thoughts, using the feedback model outlined in this chapter.

(4) After everyone has had a turn focusing on the positive, think of a person with whom you have had an *unpleasant* experience. Using the model and imagining that they are in the chair, give that person some feedback.

(5) Discuss the experience after everyone has had a turn.

HELPFUL HINTS:

Some students may feel a little uneasy at first. By modeling the desired behavior and demonstrating this activity, you might lower their anxiety level.

When students are using the feedback model to talk about an *unpleasant* experience, you may want to have them use fictitious names.

DISCUSSION:

(1) Was it easier to give feedback about a pleasant or unpleasant experience?

(2) What feedback have you received which has made a difference in your life?

(3) Who gives you the most *positive* feedback?

(4) Who gives you the most *negative* feedback?

(5) Why do many people concentrate on the *negative* things said about them?

USING FEEDBACK WITH OTHERS

Caring and Sharing 128

PURPOSE:

To give the students an opportunity to practice the feedback model in their everyday lives and to check their understanding of the model.

MATERIALS:

Paper; pencil/pen.

PROCEDURE:

(1) Review the steps of the feedback model to yourself. During a conversation with someone outside the class, use the feedback model. It may be with someone who is close to you or with someone you know only casually.

Spontaneously work the feedback response into the conversation. Make a mental note of the wording you used and the person's reactions or comments.

(2) Write a description of the experience, reporting your words and the words of the other person as closely as you can. Tell what the outcome, if any, seemed to be.

(3) Share your paper with someone else in the class who also tried the assignment.

HELPFUL HINTS:

The experience is designed to be a spontaneous one. The students work a feedback response into their conversation when it seems appropriate. Some may not get all three steps of the facilitative feedback model outlined in the chapter, but they should get at least the first two parts.

Collect the papers, read their reports and number the steps on their papers so they can see the model. Remember that the steps may be in different order. Look for any advice or evaluation and note it as *"LF"* (low facilitative, perhaps?). Put the students into groups and have them tell about their experiences.

Option: Students may write a paper about a time when they used the feedback model and spoke to their pleasant feelings and a time when they used the model to speak about their unpleasant feelings (a confrontation).

Option: Using the *Absent Person* activity, or some form of it, students can practice giving the feedback response before using it with others. Reports can then include remarks on how it was the same, and yet different, as that which was practiced in class.

DISCUSSION:

(1) Look at the feedback response and number the steps (if not done already by the trainer). In what order did they occur?

(2) Look at your choice of words. Would you use the same ones again if you were in the same situation? What changes would you make, if any?

(3) How did the conversation go after the exchange of feedback and the person's reaction. Did it flow easily? Did it get off track?

(4) Were you able to integrate a feedback response into your conversation or did you feel awkward or phony?

Activity 5.4:
STRENGTH BOMBARDMENT

PURPOSE:

To give students an opportunity to focus on positive strengths of self and others.

MATERIALS:

None.

PROCEDURE:

(1) This experience can be done in a large group, although the larger the group the fewer the number of people who can make a comment or call out a strength. It has often been used effectively with 10 participants.

(2) The participants form a semi-circle with an empty chair in front of the group.

(3) Someone volunteers to take turns in the chair. The volunteer sits there for about 1-2 minutes while the rest of the group calls out the person's positive strengths (One of the things I like about you is. . . ." "I like your. . . ." "You have a. . . .") *No put downs; no killer statements.* If negative statements are used, the trainer should interrupt and focus the group's comments on the positive. Since this rarely happens, the group has a positive experience.

(4) The group leader calls "time" and the person in the chair tells what the experience was like—a few comments—before returning to the semi-circle. Another person volunteers and another "bombardment" takes place.

(5) *Everyone takes a turn in the chair.* After everyone has taken a turn, the group talks about the experience.

HELPFUL HINTS:

This is an excellent activity for the peers to use in their group work with elementary and middle school students. The time limit makes for a rapid calling out of strengths. The person in the chair listens without talking until "time" is called. It is not necessary to use the feedback model. Brief statements can be effective. (P.S. The trainer should take a turn, too. It's fun! Enjoy it!)

Option: No time limit is used. This activity is a popular one and, depending upon the group, the time limit may need to be waived for some people. Not everyone can comment when the time limit is strictly adhered to. On the other hand, the time limit seems to encourage people to jump in and make their responses. The time limit also takes the pressure off those who may not be moved to offer a strength that they have observed.

DISCUSSION:

(1) How is this approach different than the feedback model outlined in the chapter?

(2) Where do you think this activity might be used in your work? Can you think of any variations?

Activity 5.5:
AMNESIA GAME

PURPOSE:

To help students learn more about themselves through a feedback activity.

MATERIALS: None.

PROCEDURE:

(1) A student is identified as suffering from amnesia and pretends not to know anything about the past.

(2) The rest of the group tells the person some things that will help that person to remember and become the same person as before. The group becomes specific and tells how the person typically behaved in certain situations, perhaps the reaction of others, their feelings and any other observations. For example:

    (A) favorite words and expressions
    (B) usual way of acting in class
    (C) typical way of behaving around a teacher or adult
    (D) what might be done in a certain situation

(3) The "amnesia victim" may ask questions of the group to gain more insight.

HELPFUL HINTS:

This activity is especially effective with students who have some "blind spots." Some modeling might be used. On occasion, people could be asked to try out or "practice" behaviors suggested to help "jar" the memory and help them be themselves again.

DISCUSSION:

(1) Are there some things about yourself that you think most people remember you for? Are you pleased with these behaviors or actions?

(2) If you were to step outside yourself—to see yourself as an amnesia victim—what ten things come to mind that you would remind yourself to do? To be?

Chapter VI

responsible decision - making

CHAPTER HIGHLIGHTS

(Caring and Sharing, pages 129-146)

People must continually make decisions. The myriad of alternatives now available has created a situation which causes many people to be confused and to struggle in attempts to make self-enhancing, productive decisions— decisions with which they are both pleased and proud. The relatively stable social norms of the past are in a state of transition. Therefore, decision-making has become much more complex and it also consumes more time and energy.

This chapter outlines a five-step process of making decisions. Special emphasis is placed upon the exploration and consideration of alternatives and consequences. The five steps are:

1. **Identify the central issue or problem.**

2. **Explore the issue or problem: alternatives and consequences.**

3. **Choose a next step.**

4. **Act upon your choice.**

5. **Evaluate the results.**

All people are ultimately responsible for their lives. They create and shape their own present and future through choices they consciously or unconsciously make each day. Personal responsibility is the "bottom line" in the decision-making process.

GUIDELINES FOR TRAINING

I. One interesting and thought-provoking way to begin looking at the decision-making process is to have the students write their reactions to the opening quote: *"Not to decide, is to decide."* A class discussion might follow.

II. Examining the alternatives and the consequences surrounding any decision is, perhaps, the most crucial step in making a decision. There are a number of approaches which can be used to heighten students' awareness. One method is to discourage the use of the words, "I can't. . ." and replace them with the phrase, "I choose not to, at this point in my life." This tends to emphasize the reality that there *are* alternatives available. Students see themselves as responsible for what happens in their lives. They sense more of their own "personal power" and realize that they have numerous opportunities to shape and brighten their own lives—if only they *choose* to use their power.

III. Decision-making is the "bedrock" of the values clarification approach (e.g. Raths, Simon and Harmin in *Values and Teaching*, 1966). This might be an opportune time to outline the basic tenets of this approach and to have the students experience a number of the enjoyable and stimulating values clarification strategies. Activities such as *Rank Orders, Forced Choices, Continuums* and *List-making* all contribute to helping clarify what is prized and cherished by a person. Also, many of these same strategies might then be used by the facilitators themselves when they are working with others.

IV. Decision-making involves the use of both the *cognitive* and *affective* domains. Yet, many people stress only the cognitive aspects and ignore or overlook the feelings that influence a decision. Questions such as: "How would you feel if that happened?" or "How are you feeling as we talk about this decision you are about to make?" can assist students to see that there is a distinct relationship between *thinking* and *feeling*.

V. Demonstrate a "decision-making session." You might do this by asking for a student to volunteer for a "counseling" demonstration with you. Put the rest of the group in a circle, with you and the volunteer seated in the middle. Discuss the topic: "What is one decision you are attempting to make in your life right now?"

Help the volunteer outline the major components of the decision. Proceed to use high facilitative responses as you help the person explore alternatives and possible consequences. At the end of the demonstration, have a class discussion on what the facilitators observed.

SETTING PRIORITIES

Caring and Sharing   144

PURPOSE:

To practice the skill of decision-making by becoming more aware of alternatives and values.

MATERIALS:

None.

PROCEDURE:

Look at each of the following rank ordered questions. Write a No. 1 to indicate your top priority, a No. 2 for your second priority and a No. 3 for your lowest priority:

A. What is the most important characteristic that your boy/girl friend can possess?

_____ good-looking

_____ fun at parties

_____ intelligent

B. Where would you rather be on a Saturday afternoon?

_____ watching a sports program on T.V.

_____ at the beach

_____ on a picnic with your family

C. What is the one thing about school that you would really like to see changed?

_____ the grading system

_____ going five days a week

_____ the teachers

D. Which would you "least" like to be?

_____ very poor

_____ confined to a wheelchair

_____ blind

E. Which would you give up, if you had to?

_____ religious freedom

_____ economic freedom

_____ political freedom

HELPFUL HINTS:

More involvement might be generated by developing your own rank orders out of the issues which seem most relevant to your own setting. For example, you could have the students rank order three qualities that they would value in choosing a college: (a) located close to home; (b) has a good reputation; (c) the student/teacher ratio is very low.

Or you could add a fourth and fifth alternative to each rank order and then have them set their priorities.

DISCUSSION:

(1) What priorities in your own life do you have the most difficulty in rank ordering?

(2) What can you do to increase the probability that you will be aware of all of the alternatives available to you in any situation?

(3) What are the three highest priorities in your life right now? How did you come to value these three over others?

GOOD DECISIONS—POOR DECISIONS

Caring and Sharing 145

PURPOSE:

To further explore the decision-making process; to look at the consequences of our decisions.

MATERIALS:

Notes About Me notebook; pencil/pen.

PROCEDURE:

(1) Divide one page of your notebook in half. Mark the top half of the page "Good Decisions." Mark the words "Poor Decisions" on the bottom section.

(2) Thinking back over some important decisions you have made during the past six months, categorize them according to results. Write key words describing the decision in the appropriate section.

(3) Look at the "Good Decisions" section. Ask yourself the following questions:

    A. How did I come to make these decisions?

    B. Who was influential in my making the decision?

    C. How many of these decisions were the result of my having received advice from others?

(4) Ask these same questions as you look at the "Poor Decisions" section.

(5) Now, write down your impressions of this activity. What did you learn or relearn?

HELPFUL HINTS:

Remind the students to consider decisions that they have made at school, at home, in relation to their friends, at their job and so forth. You may need to provide some examples in order to get them thinking and recalling.

DISCUSSION:

(1) How responsible are we for determining our futures? What about a person who is born into poverty? Or handicapped? Or who is a victim of abusive parents?

(2) Compare the process of decision-making outlined in *Caring and Sharing* with the philosophy of "Live for Today."

(3) Do we have to give up our spontaneity in order to be responsible decision-makers?

WESTERN UNION
Caring and Sharing   146

PURPOSE:

To illustrate one means of taking a stand and acting upon somthing that is important to you.

MATERIALS:

A 3" x 5" index card or a Western Union telegram form; pencil/-pen.

PROCEDURE:

(1) Design a Western Union form according to the model in *Caring and Sharing.*

(2) Complete the form using a real-life situation which you feel is important.

(3) Read the telegram in class and/or send it to the person involved.

HELPFUL HINTS:

Be sure to discuss the possible consequences of sending a Western Union telegram. Assist the students to learn that putting their views in writing often calls for a greater commitment.

DISCUSSION:

(1) How many times have you ever seen anyone actually *do something* about someone's concern?

(2) What are the differences between those who complain and those who act to change the situation?

(3) What issues at this school need to be brought to the attention of the administration/parents via a telegram?

(4) What are the consequences of being viewed as "complainer" or "radical?"

(5) What if you sent such a telegram to (a) your parents; (b) a teacher; and (c) a friend. What would you urge them to do?

THE VOLUNTEER EXPERIENCE

PURPOSE:

To help students clarify the inner conflicts that are a part of decision-making.

MATERIALS:

None.

PROCEDURE:

(1) Begin by saying something like this: "Okay, I'm going to need a volunteer to come from the group and work with me on a new activity. I've been thinking about this activity for a long time now, but I haven't used it with you. It won't take very long, but I'm going to need some help."

(2) Then say: "Well, I don't really need a volunteer, but I would like for all of you to close your eyes and focus on the experience you just had when I called for a volunteer to help me— focus on those few moments when you were trying to decide whether or not to be that volunteer."

(3) Continue by saying: "Imagine that you have two of you inside your head. One of them wants you to volunteer, while the other is against it. What are they saying to you as they try to convince you what to do? How do the voices sound?"

(4) Continue by saying: "Now have each of them try to convince you what to do, but there are no words. What actions are they using? Who seems to be winning?

(5) Continuing: "Open your eyes. Let's talk about what you experienced. Someone tell us what happened to you."

HELPFUL HINTS:

This activity illustrates the conflict that most of us experience when asked to volunteer, even though some readily make a decision one way or another. Encourage the group to share their thoughts while you summarize themes, clarify and make high facilitative responses. In this sense, you are modeling. There's no need to interpret any special symbols or actions. No evaluation or advice. As members listen to one another, similar experiences will be evident, such as familiar arguments for and against volunteering. This can be a reassuring experience for some as they hear that others have similar "unconscious conflicts." This might be related to other situations, especially when they are encouraging someone to volunteer some information.

DISCUSSION:

(1) How is this experience related to other situations in the classroom? In response to a speaker's call for questions from an audience? Going into the military service? Being a candidate for student council?

(2) Is it the number of arguments or the kind of argument that convinces you most of what to do? How many decisions have you made where you sat down and listed the pro and con arguments that play in the decision?

(3) Which "unconscious person" tends to win out the most? The one that says "Yes" or the one that is saying "No, don't do it!"?

(4) What did you learn about yourself from this experience?

PERSONAL CONTRACT

PURPOSE:

To commit yourself to a plan of action and make a decision. To provide a "support system" as you seek to achieve a goal you've set.

MATERIALS:

Pen/pencil.

PROCEDURE:

(1) Decide upon a realistic, achievable goal that you'd like to attain in the next two or three months. This goal may be related to a change in your behavior, your attitudes or any other area you choose.

(2) Reproduce the contract from page 80 and distribute it to the students for completion. Carefully consider each section.

(3) Now, decide who you would like to "co-sign" your contract. The co-signer must agree to support your efforts. Also, they might share in your "celebration ceremony."

(4) Together, set aside a time each week to review your progress.

HELPFUL HINTS:

Have the students give a copy of their contract to their co-signers. This will help insure that no misunderstandings occur. Periodically, take 5-10 minutes and have the students give quick reports on how they are progressing in relation to keeping their contracts.

DISCUSSION:

(1) How many of you make a list of New Year's resolutions each January ? How successful have you been in achieving these goals?

(2) What is your response to the following quote: "When everything is said and done, there's usually more *said* than *done*!"?

(3) What makes it so difficult for many people to change their behavior—even when they say they truly want to change?

(4) What are some other goals that you might write on another contract?

PERSONAL CONTRACT

I, _____(your name)_____,
being of superb mind and body, hereby resolve to achieve
the following:

_____

_____
_____
_____

I plan to achieve this by _____(date)_____.
When I accomplish my goal, there will be the following
celebration ceremony:

_____
_____

_____   _____
(your signature)   (date)

_____   _____
(signature of co-signer) (date)

Chapter VII

assessing self and others

CHAPTER HIGHLIGHTS

(Caring and Sharing, pages 147-164)

This chapter is divided into three parts. The first part focuses on *assessment of self*. Students are encouraged to think about themselves, their values and self-pictures. A *Self-appraisal Inventory* is provided to assist them in their assessment.

The next section emphasizes the importance of *assessing the helping process*. It suggests that facilitators must be responsible for what they do. One way of being more responsible is to take account of the skills and techniques used in working with others. A *Facilitative Skills Checklist* is included in the chapter. Students are asked to share their responses with each other.

Finally, attention is given to *assessing the outcomes of peer intervention*. General and specific goals are discussed, as well as some different approaches to evaluation. In particular, the *Systematic Case Study* is described as one approach in which peer facilitators can evaluate their efforts with either individuals or groups.

GUIDELINES FOR TRAINING

I. Evaluation can be a threatening experience. It need not be. It is important for the trainer to help students recognize the value of assessing their work. This includes looking at the skills they use and their personality—which is a part of the process. Other instruments might be used to help students look at themselves, including standardized personality inventories which might be available through the guidance office. If students have progressed through the chapters and activities outlined in this book, they should be more open to self-examination at this point. Nevertheless, the trainer's attitude can influence the depth of exploration and assessment.

II. The *Facilitative Skills Checklist* is one way for students to examine their work. It can be applied to a specific case or situation or it may be used as an overall assessment of one's work. In addition, it might be used for assessing the process with an individual or group. Students may want to add other items or to clarify the significance of a particular item. Encourage them to do so.

III. While several methods might be used to help evaluate peer intervention outcomes, some peer facilitator trainers have found it most helpful to single out one or two approaches that might be given priority. The *Systematic Case Study* is a relatively simple procedure that can provide valuable information. It not only helps peers to evaluate their work, but it also gives them an opportunity to gain some personal satisfaction. Most important, it can be used to make timely adjustments where needed.

All evaluation instruments have their limitations. Likewise, so do the different methods of evaluation. The important thing is to help peer facilitators gain a better understanding of themselves and their work. The more systematic the effort, the more opportunity there is for positive gains and recognition.

IV. Trainers might use any of the methods, but especially the *Systematic Case Approach*, as one way of collecting information about the effectiveness of the peer facilitator program. Identifying data can be changed or omitted and the case studies can be briefly described to show the impact that peer facilitator work has on other students.

V. Public relations is an important part of gaining support. The more support that is present, the more opportunities there are for peer intervention. The ideas in this chapter may be used to collect data for a public relations effort. By thinking and planning ahead, it is possible to avoid the often expressed lament: "I wish I had. . ." or "If only we had. . . ."

Activity 7.1:
SELF-EVALUATION

Caring and Sharing   162

PURPOSE:

To provide a means of clarifying and reinforcing what was gained from a particualr activity/experience; a means of achieving closure.

MATERIALS:

None.

PROCEDURE:

(1) After any activity that you do in class and/or any experience that you have, write some of the following statements in your *Notes to Myself:*

> A. I learned that I. . . .
>
> B. I relearned that I. . . .
>
> C. I realized that I. . . .
>
> D. I was displeased that I. . . .
>
> E. I discovered that I. . . .
>
> F. I wonder. . . .

(2) *Share your responses with the class or pair up with another person and discuss your reactions.*

HELPFUL HINTS:

This activity is an excellent way of getting your students to further explore and think about their experiences. This "private processing" is a time for learning and understanding. Use this activity whenever you sense that your students could profit from more introspection.

Also, the verbal sharing of responses to these unfinished sentences enables them to summarize their learnings at the end of each week. You can learn more about what the students gained from your efforts the previous five days, plus they hear what their classmates learned.

DISCUSSION:

(1) What causes individuals to perceive events in totally different ways?

(2) What is so important about learning about yourself?

(3) How do people learn?

(4) What makes some events more important than others?

WHAT MAKES SUCCESS?

PURPOSE:

To focus on some positive aspects of yourself; to share accomplishments; and to practice listening.

MATERIALS:

Pieces of paper (8$\frac{1}{2}$" x 11"); pencil/pen.

PROCEDURE:

(1) Divide your paper by drawing a vertical line down the center.

(2) Title the left column "Accomplishments." Title the right column "Action."

(3) Now, in order, list the following in the "Accomplishments" column:

> A. One thing you accomplished while in elementary school.

> B. One thing you accomplished while in junior high or middle school.

> C. One thing you have accomplished recently.

> D. One thing you hope to accomplish in the near future.

(4) Examine each of your accomplishments. Think about what you did to be successful. There were probably many small things that contributed to your success. Write two behaviors or actions that helped you achieve each of your accomplishments.

(5) After your list is complete, form a small group and share your accomplishments. Then, tell what actions contributed to each success.

(6) After everyone has shared, discuss your reactions. Share your thoughts about such things as:

> A. What general themes did you hear?

> B. Were some of the actions the same?

> C. Are your past accomplishments related to what you hope to accomplish in the future?

HELPFUL HINTS:

Students may want you to clarify the meaning of the word "accomplishment." Stress that the important factor is that *they* consider whatever they have done as an accomplishment. It matters not whether others would categorize it as a major or minor accomplishment. Help students think of some behaviors/actions that were influential in achieving their goals.

DISCUSSION:

(1) How do you decide what accomplishments you wish to achieve?

(2) Finish the following: "Success is . . . ."

(3) Name two people you personally know whom you consider successful. What personal characteristics have helped them be so successful?

Activity 7.3:
PLANNING A CASE STUDY
Caring and Sharing 164

PURPOSE:

To practice the steps involved in planning a case study.

MATERIALS: Paper and pencil/pen.

PROCEDURE:

(1) Form a group of three.

(2) Turn to *The Systematic Case Study* (*Caring and Sharing*, page 160).

(3) As a group, decide upon an imaginary person or group of people that you would like to help.

(4) Cooperatively, plan a systematic case study for that person or group. Be sure to give attention to each part of the study: baseline data, intervention and so forth.

(5) After your group has developed a plan, share it with another group. This group will help you critique your efforts.

(6) Make a list of three things that would be needed before you could put the plan into action.

HELPFUL HINTS:

Conducting a case study will be a new task for almost all peer facilitators. Be as specific as possible. Outline what is expected of them. You may want to hand each group a copy of a previously-completed study to use as a model. Another alternative is to first do a sample case study on the chalkboard.

You may need to have a brainstorming session related to an imaginary person or group of people that you would like to help.

DISCUSSION:

(1) How do you determine if/when a person or a group of persons needs your help? What criteria would you use?

(2) What are some reasons for conducting a case study? How could such a study help our program?

(3) What can be proven by conducting a case study?

PEOPLE SCAVENGER HUNT

PURPOSE:

To get to know each other better and have fun.

MATERIALS:

Individual copies of the questions below; pencil/pen.

PROCEDURE:

(1) Give each student a copy of the questions below.

(2) Students are to find someone for as many categories as possible.

(3) At the end of 20 minutes, have the students share their results in groups of six.

Find someone who. . .

_____ 1.   watches less than 5 hours of TV each week.
How do they spend their time?

_____ 2.   jogs at least 10 miles each week.
What do they think about as they jog?

_____ 3.   thinks sporting events at school are a waste of time.
What are their reasons?

_____ 4.   loves to read mystery novels.
Have them tell you about their favorite.

_____ 5.   has ever considered running away from home.
Where were they going to go?

_____ 6.   would like to write a book.
What would be the title?

_____ 7.   would like a temple rub.
Rub-a-dub-dub....

_____ 8.   has disappointing grades this year.
Have that person sit on your lap while telling about it.

_____ 9.   feels that the legal drinking age should be lowered to sixteen.
Have them give you three reasons.

_____ 10   enjoys being with their parent(s).
Have them tell you what makes their parent(s) so special.

_____ 11.   has attended a funeral in the past year.
Have them share their feelings about the experience.

HELPFUL HINTS:

This can be a fun activity and a good mixer. You might say something like: "Look over the list that I just passed out. You will find some very interesting items. You will have 20 minutes in which to move around and talk with people in the group, trying to find someone who meets the criteria for each item. Get the information "first-hand" and don't copy from others. Have fun and find out what you can about the group." No other ground rules seem to be needed. Let the group use the time in any way that they wish to gather the people's names. You might want to do this activity in an area with some privacy or where there is a lot of space for moving around.

DISCUSSION:

(1) How much time did you spend with each individual? What prompted you to spend more time with one person than another?

(2) How competitive were you? Did you find yourself wanting to move to another person because of the "game" or were there times when you wanted to give up the game and talk with the person longer?

(3) What was the most interesting thing you learned? Were there any surprises?

(4) Which questions were the most uncomfortable to ask? Which ones were the easiest?

(5) Did you spend most of your time interviewing or being interviewed?

(6) What would you do differently next time?

(7) Make up three "scavenger hunt" categories of your own that you'd like to add to the list.

HOW DO I RESPOND?

PURPOSE:

To help students analyze their verbal interactions with others.

MATERIALS:

Tape recorder; blank tape; paper and pencil/pen.

PROCEDURE:

(1) Each student is to be given an opportunity to talk with another person for about 10 minutes while acting as a facilitator. The interview or discussion is tape recorded.

(2) The topic may be of the facilitator or talker's choosing, the following might be interesting:

    (a) Athletics and Our School
    (b) My Family and Its Traditions
    (c) Sex Role Stereotyping

(3) Following the interview, the student serving as a facilitator then listens to the tape and, using a pen or pencil, records each statement word for word and in sequence, as taken off the tape. Thus, a list of the facilitator's statements is compiled.

(4) The student will then:

    (a) Classify each statement according to the *Continuum of Facilitative Responses.* A question mark is used to designate those that the facilitator has difficulty categorizing.

    (b) Tally the number of responses for each of the six categories.

(5) Have the facilitator discuss with the talker the impact of certain statements and write a concluding statement about what was learned from the experience.

HELPFUL HINTS:

This excercise will help students examine "the process" of facilitating others. It gives attention to the facilitator's responses only. Even though examined out of context, it enables the facilitator to gain a picture of the overall response pattern.

Make sure the persons being taped have given their permission.

DISCUSSION:

(1) What did you learn about being a facilitator from this activity?

(2) What kind of responses did you tend to use the most?

(3) Was there a pattern in your reponses? At what point did the most number of questions occur? Feeling responses?

(4) Were there any statements that you'd like to change? Which ones? Edit them on your paper, as you would like to have said them.

(5) What are three feeling words that describe how you felt while being the facilitator? What are three words that describe how you felt after you looked at your recorded statements?

Chapter VIII

getting ready to help others

CHAPTER HIGHLIGHTS

(Caring and Sharing, pages 165-198)

This chapter focuses on some of the practical aspects of being a peer facilitator. The roles of *tutor, big brother/ sister* and *group discussion leader* are outlined. A number of case studies are presented which amplify and clarify some approaches that peer facilitators have used in fulfilling these roles.

Planning notes for a *Self-Awareness Group* are presented, as well as an outline for a *Communications Lab.* The "feelings classes" approach, outlined by Joe Wittmer and Robert Myrick, is discussed in detail. Programmed approaches to counseling, such as the *Vocational Exploration Group (VEG)* and the *Developing Understanding of Self and Others (DUSO)*, are mentioned as ways in which peer facilitators can supplement professional counselors in a school.

Some other settings where peer facilitators have worked (e.g. retirement centers, hospitals) are briefly described. The chapter ends with a number of suggestions made by veteran peer facilitators.

GUIDELINES FOR TRAINING

I. This is usually a time when some of the facilitators begin to question and doubt their ability to help others. Some may begin to challenge some of the concepts taught earlier and openly state their frustration and concern about what you are expecting them to do. Their reading about the experiences of other facilitators may result in your having to respond to: "I can't do the things you are asking of me. I don't know what to say or which activities to use. I don't even understand what we're really trying to accomplish in here."

Use your counseling and consultation skills. Be empathic. Be aware of the tendency to respond only with reassuring and supportive statements. Their feelings of anxiety and doubt require your sensitivity and patience.

You could have students anonymously write down their feelings and questions after reading Chapter VIII. This could help you get a sense of how training is progressing.

II. After the facilitators have a relatively clear understanding of the three roles, or any other roles you have presented, you may want to have them "rank order" these roles. This ranking might be based upon which role they feel most comfortable fulfilling and in what setting. Some facilitators may choose to be a tutor during the elementary phase and then a group discussion leader when working with older students. The rank ordering helps them to be clear and concrete when making their commitment to a role.

III. Several structured experiences and activities have been presented and a resulting concern is that the facilitator will see these activities as the "goal"—that doing an activity will automatically result in success.

Facilitators must understand that *all activities are only a means by which to generate feelings, opinions, ideas and questions.* The critical step, then, is to *process* these feelings, opinions, ideas and questions by using the skills presented earlier (listening, responding, decision-making and feedback).

Activities are used as a catalyst—a means to stimulate and personally involve the participants. The ideas and feelings generated by the activity are the real food for thought.

IV. This may be an excellent time to have the facilitators conduct a *Needs Assessment* related to the various social service agencies in your community and the services they provide. This may assist you in determining alternative settings for the facilitators.

Activity 8.1:

PREPARING FOR YOUR FIRST ASSIGNMENT
Caring and Sharing   196

PURPOSE:

To insure that the students have planned adequately for their first experience as a peer facilitator and to increase their self-confidence.

MATERIALS:

None.

PROCEDURE:

(1) Know your asssignment ! Be clear on your role. What is expected of you? Obtain some general information about the person(s) with whom you will work.

(2) Answer the following questions *before* beginning your work:

> A. What are the goals? What are you trying to accomplish?

> B. What can the participant(s) expect to gain by cooperating with you?

> C. What are two or three possible problems you may confront? How would you attempt to resolve each of these problems?

> D. What are two or three activities that you feel would be appropriate for your first session? What stimulating questions can you ask?

(3) Share your ideas with a partner.

HELPFUL HINTS:

Be sure to have done your own "homework" before the students begin asking you for the specifics of their first assignment. By having carefully planned and organized this first assignment, you will be laying an important foundation upon which to build future successful experiences.

You may want to have the students respond to the questions in writing and turn their papers into you. This will give you some idea of how "ready" your students really are.

DISCUSSION:

(1) What words would you use to describe how you felt as you answered these questions?

(2) Complete five *I wonder. . .* statements related to your first assignment.

Activity 8.2:
GETTING READY
Caring and Sharing 197

PURPOSE:

To begin planning for a peer facilitator intervention.

MATERIALS:

Notes to Myself notebook; paper and pencil/pen.

PROCEDURE:

(1) Review your *Notes to Myself* notebook, this text and any other materials that you believe will be helpful in planning an intervention.

(2) Identify your five favorite activities—activities that you would like to use with others.

(3) Review these activities; take note of the procedures and add any comments that you believe will be helpful.

(4) Next, place the activities in order (one to five) that you think would be feasible.

(5) In addition, develop some interesting questions for each of the activities. Make some notes that will help you proceed with the activity.

(6) Now, share your plan with someone else in the class. Encourage them to help you critique the plan.

(7) What three things are needed before you can put the plan (the sequence of activities) into action?

HELPFUL HINTS:

This is an important activity for facilitators to complete. Through reviewing their notes and prioritizing the activities, they will have a better understanding of what they are trying to accomplish and how they plan to do it.

Facilitators may need your assistance in modifying certain activities to *fit* the age and maturity level of the students with whom they are working.

DISCUSSION:

(1) What do you hope that students will learn from experiencing the activities you've chosen?

(2) Do your activities call for more writing, talking or physical activity?

(3) What could you do to make these activities relate to the *real world* of the students with whom you use them?

ACOUNTABILITY LOG
Caring and Sharing   198

PURPOSE:

To maintain a record of your experiences as a peer facilitator; to assist in planning.

MATERIALS:

A spiral notebook or stenographer's pad.

PROCEDURE:

(1) Following each activity which you facilitate, make an entry which includes the following points:

A. Date of activity.

B. Time spent on activity.

C. Who participated.

D. Name of activity/experience.

E. Your impressions of how the activity went.

F. Important statements made by the participants.

G. What you feel would be a good activity for the next meeting.

(2) Discuss your entry with another person in the class.

HELPFUL HINTS:

These logs are an excellent means for you to stay in touch with what is happening in the program. By reading these logs (perhaps once a week or every two weeks), you can get a sense of who may need your help, who may be getting frustrated and who is doing an outstanding job.

Using clarifying responses and providing alternatives from which to choose have proven to be the most effective ways of responding to the information in these logs. Avoid grading the logs.

DISCUSSION:

None.

Activity 8.4:
FIRST IMPRESSIONS

PURPOSE:

To help students think about the kind of initial impressions that they make and the importance of first impressions.

MATERIALS:

Paper and pencil/pen.

PROCEDURE:

(1) Students list five *first impressions* that they believe others generally have of them in a first meeting. *What are some of the things people first notice about you? List five.*

(2) Divide the class into small discussion groups.

(3) Since the group probably knows each other at this point, they are asked to look around the group and write one first impression that they *had* or believe that others *would have* about each person in the group.

(4) One person volunteers to hear what the others have written. Others in the group, in turn and in a go-around, read the impression that they wrote down about the volunteer.

(5) As the volunteer hears what others say, that person makes a note of each statement and later compares what others have said to the five items recorded.

(6) After each person has taken a turn, members examine their own lists and compare them with the list made from the groups' comments.

HELPFUL HINTS:

This activity can help students think about what they do and do not do when they first meet people. It also will help them learn what others believe are the first things people learn about them. Following this experience, you can help students think about first impressions that they may make on (a) their host in the field experience and (b) the student(s) with whom they will work.

DISCUSSION:

(1) What themes do you see in each of the lists?

(2) How is your list the same and different from what others said?

(3) What seems to be the *consensus* about the most prominent first impression.

(4) Do you make different *first impressions* with some people than others?

(5) What part does the setting or the situation play in determining the first impression you make?

(6) Are your first impressions with adults different from first impressions with students? Does age level make a difference?

Activity 8.5:
THE APPLICATION

PURPOSE:

To help students examine their skills as a peer facilitator.

MATERIALS:

Application Form; pencil/pen.

PROCEDURE:

Give each student a dittoed sheet of paper that is made to look like an application form. It should contain the following information:

APPLICATION FORM

Name of Host _____

Peer Facilitator's Name _____

Field Experience Setting _____

I would like to be a peer facilitator in your (class or setting).

I believe that I'll be successful because:

(1) _____

(2) _____

(3) _____

However, I think that you should also know that I am:

(4) _____

(5) _____

(6) _____

Thank you. I am looking forward to your prompt reply.

Sincerely yours,

_____
(facilitator's name)

HELPFUL HINTS:

This is a fun activity that can also be used to stimulate some feedback to students. There are several ways to use this activity. You might divide the class into small groups and have the members put their forms into a secret pool. Students take turns drawing them out and guessing who wrote the application form or have each person read their own application form and obtain feedback from other members in the group regarding items 1, 2 and 3. You may want to have the students add and delete something from the form.

DISCUSSION:

(1) What things do you think a host will want to know about you?

(2) What are some things on the application form that you would feel comfortable sharing with the person with whom you're working? Uncomfortable?

(3) What theme(s) appear when you look at items 4 5 and 6? Same or different?

Chapter IX

problem moments

CHAPTER HIGHLIGHTS
(Caring and Sharing, pages 199-214)

Problem moments are part of being a peer facilitator. In this chapter some concerns expressed by other students are presented. A brief response is given. The problem moments lend themselves to further discussion.

GUIDELINES FOR TRAINING

I. Students will share their problem moments, as well as their successful ones, when they feel they are part of an open and accepting group. A few students will feel that they must be "perfect" and will try to hide their concerns. This chapter is designed to encourage students to think about the problems that they, or others, are having. It is more reassuring and productive to hear about problems and talk about them openly, rather than dismiss their importance by suggesting that everything will "turn out all right" and that they shouldn't worry.

II. When exploring problem moments, it can be helpful to first understand the feelings that are present and then examine how those feelings are affecting a person's behavior. Several feelings might be present, including some ambivalent ones.

III. Before rushing to a solution, trainers are encouraged to make the problem moment a learning experience. Be a good listener. Model the facilitative skills, including the feedback model. Let others respond before jumping in with a quick answer. With experience, most trainers discover simple and quick solutions to many problems. However, the more experienced and effective trainers will do what they can to provide quality work settings and, when problems arise, they will take the time that is necessary to give them some careful thought.

It is important that time be given to a discussion of the first problems that arise. Students then learn a decision-making process that may later make them less dependent upon the trainer or class for support.

IV. Finally, while this chapter focuses on *problem moments*, it is important to remember that time could also be set aside for giving attention to *rewarding moments*. Sometimes an activity can be arranged in which each student can talk about something that has been rewarding and something that has been dissatisfying. In addition to an interesting class discussion, the sharing of problem moments and moments of satisfaction can also build group cohesiveness.

Activity 9.1:
HOW I HANDLE MY PROBLEMS
Caring and Sharing 210

PURPOSE:

To explore past experiences in resolving problems.

MATERIALS:

None.

PROCEDURE:

(1) Think about some problem situations which have confronted you during the past year.

(2) Fill in the chart (*Caring and Sharing,* page 210).

(3) Complete the following unfinished sentences:

    A. When confronted with a major problem, I....

    B. My problems are usually caused by....

    C. In order to become more successful at resolving my problems, I need to....

(4) Share your responses in trios.

HELPFUL HINTS:

Explain that the problems didn't have to be major problems. Use this to explore both relatively minor as well as major problems. If a "final outcome" has not been achieved as yet, have the facilitators write the current status of the problem. They may also want to hypothesize about the problem outcome.

DISCUSSION:

(1) What are two or three main sources of your problems. . . school, home life, the opposite sex, yourself and so forth?

(2) When you are having problems, how does it affect you at school?

(3) Respond to the statement, "It is sometimes helpful to feel sorry for myself. It gets me to explore who I really am."

WHAT SHOULD BE DONE NOW ?
Caring and Sharing 211

PURPOSE:

To examine some problem moments that other facilitators have had.

MATERIALS:

The problem moments presented in *Caring and Sharing.*

PROCEDURE:

(1) Read a problem moment. Imagine what you would do if you were in this situation.

(2) Write a response that illustrates what you might do first, then next and so on. If it is a response, then put quotation marks around your words.

(3) Get in a small group and have someone read a problem moment aloud. Then the people in the group tell what they would do. Be sure to read or say your responses aloud.

HELPFUL HINTS:

Having the peer facilitators share their possible solutions to each problem moment can be threatening and anxiety-producing. Caution the facilitators not to "sit in judgment" of each other as they explore possible responses/approaches. Rather, encourage them to keep an open mind as they listen to the suggestions of others.

Option: Role play each of these problem moments.

DISCUSSION:

(1) How were you feeling as you read each problem moment?

(2) Rank order the six situations. Make the No. 1 situation the one that you feel would be the most difficult for you to handle.

ROLE PLAYING
Caring and Sharing 214

PURPOSE:

To identify problem moments and role play possible responses.

MATERIALS:

Paper and pencil; any chairs or props that are appropriate for role playing situations.

PROCEDURE:

(1) The class is divided into three groups. Each group writes two problem moments, one for each of the other two groups.

(2) Each team then takes the two new problem moments and discusses among themselves how they will act out the problem. A "script" may be written which presents the key issues involved.

(3) Each team, in turn, role plays or acts out the problem moment. Allow about two to three minutes for each situation.

(4) Discussion follows regarding a) effectiveness and b) alternatives.

HELPFUL HINTS:

Emphasize that the problem moments are to be examples of those that peer facilitators might experience in their efforts to help others. You may want to provide some options for consideration such as:

(a) a teacher who asks you to dress more appropriately.

(b) an elementary student who starts to cry whenever you want that student to leave the class with you.

(c) a fellow peer facilitator who isn't really trying to do a good job.

Focus the initial discussion on how would each of you feel if you were confronted with this situation. Then, progress to an exploration of possible alternatives and the consequences of each alternative.

DISCUSSION:

(1) What other problems might you have to face as a peer facilitator?

(2) Rank order the problems discussed with No. 1 being the potential problem that most concerns you.

(3) Under what circumstances would you come to me (the trainer) and ask me to intervene in a problem you were facing?

Activity 9.4:
DEAR ABBY

PURPOSE:

To identify and discuss problems that young people often have and to recognize how feelings and behaviors are related.

MATERIALS:

Identical small slips of paper and pencils for group members.

PROCEDURE:

(1) The activity may be introduced by bringing to the class a sample of the syndicated column *Dear Abby*, or some similar feature. Emphasize how people want to get answers, but that many use the column to get things off their mind, to vent their feelings and to take a stand.

(2) Read a problem from *Abby* and then ask for possible answers. After some discussion, tell the group that you are going to introduce them to another version of *Dear Abby*.

(3) Distribute slips of paper and say: "Write down a question or a problem that you are having. If nothing comes to mind, write down a problem that a friend of yours is having. Perhaps you may just want to write down a problem that you think people your age are having and that would be interesting to discuss."

Students do not sign their names. Papers are collected and mixed.

(4) The leader draws a slip of paper from the collection and reads the problem aloud. (Note: If the leader reads from the original slips, it has the advantage of allowing for some editing in order to secure anonymity.)

(5) After the problem is read, the group first tries to imagine how it would *feel* to have a problem like that. Feeling words are suggested. Next the group is asked: "Well, if you had a feeling(s) like that, how would you behave? What kinds of things would you do to show that the feelings are there?"

HELPFUL HINTS:

Feelings and behavior are shown as being related. It is not necessary to actually answer the question or solve the problem. While suggestions may be interesting, they may also take away from the primary focus of feelings and behavior. Perhaps after the first two or three are discussed without an emphasis on "what would you do," those that follow might receive that attention. Then, some attention could be given to alternatives and consequences. The primary goal is to increase understanding and respect, not find a solution to the problem.

DISCUSSION:

(1) Is *Dear Abby* a facilitator? Considering the ideas you've read in this book, is she a facilitator? How is Abby helpful and not helpful in her column?

(2) What makes the column so popular? Would you want to be *Dear Abby*? What problems does she have when answering the letters?

IN TIMES OF STRESS

PURPOSE:

To help students learn more about who other students turn to when they have problems.

MATERIALS:

Paper; pencil; ditto to make a survey form.

PROCEDURE:

(1) Divide the class into three or four groups. Each group will develop their own survey form and will conduct a survey among students in the school.

(2) After the groups have been divided, each group is given the follownning tasks:

(a) As a group, write four problems that a student (boy or girl) might have, one for each of the following areas: social, academic, personal and relationship. Each problem must be written briefly—three or four sentence limit.

(b) Each member of the group will copy these four problem moments so they can be read verbatim.

(c) Next, each member will interview 10 students in school, read to them four problem moments and ask them to recommend someone this person might see.

Option: You might give the students a list of "possible helpers" to rank order (e.g. teacher, parent, student, counselor, minister, nobody).

(3) After students have completed their 10 interviews and collected their information, they will again meet groups. Have them share what they learned and, as a group, tally their findings. Have each group give a report to the class. One person can be identified as the recorder and reporter.

(4) After all reports are given, pool all data for one final tally.

HELPFUL HINTS:

This can be an interesting and fun activity. Help the students be specific when they develop their problem moments. Help them eliminate sexist language so that both boys and girls might respond.

It might be necessary to develop a form for boys and one for girls. If the open-ended option is used, then students are encouraged to write down the response they receive. If the second option is used (providing a list of possible choices), then students act as recorders and mark the rankings. This survey might be used to help them gain more insight as to who their peers tend to turn to in times of stress. The class then might take the survey form themselves.

DISCUSSION:

(1) What did you learn from tallying the responses? Were there any surprises in your findings?

(2) Did boys differ form girls? Older students from younger students?

(3) What types of people did the students indicate that they would see?

(4) Does the kind of problem (social, personal, academic, relationship) make a difference?

(5) How would you respond? How are you the same or different from others based on the findings reported in your group?

(6) What determines who people might turn to when they have a problem?

(7) Is this survey something that could be described in an article for the school newspaper? Who should see the results of the survey?

Chapter X

getting organized

There is no way to prevent students from helping other students. They talk with each other. They work with each other. They share their thoughts and feelings as part of "going to school." However, when peers are given more structured opportunities to learn about themselves and others and when they are given a chance to be part of an organized peer facilitator program, then an even more positive impact can take place. How can a peer facilitator program be developed? How should it be organized? What special considerations need attention?

ORGANIZING PEER FACILITATOR PROGRAMS

One of the first questions that must be answered is: "What format or organization will be used to provide the training for peer facilitators?" There are at least three available options which will help you structure the learning experience:

(1) *Peer Facilitator Clubs*

(2) *Peer Facilitator Aides*

(3) *Peer Facilitator Classes*

The first two are frequently used as a beginning point for those that are just starting an organized program. They give trainers an opportunity to experiment with ideas and time to develop their plans. The third option, a peer facilitator class, is the most extensive and exciting, but it requires more planning and commitment. Let's look at these options.

PEER FACILITATOR CLUBS

One method of organizing a peer facilitator program is to have a club. Participants meet during times that are regularly scheduled for club meetings. They use their meetings to develop helping skills and learn from each other. They then volunteer to spend a part of each week using their new skills in settings such as those described in Chapter VIII of *Caring and Sharing: Becoming a Peer Facilitator.*

A club may begin with three or four students. As it becomes larger, officers can be elected and the group can become one of the service organizations in the school/community. The club name could reflect the purpose of the group. The trainer could have a "lesson" (or discuss one chapter) for each meeting until the members reach a certain degree of competence. Members may then decide upon a project that involves the use of their skills as peer facilitators.

For example, one club decided to volunteer its members to the teachers for tutoring, while another club set a schedule of times when facilitators would be available in the school's guidance office. These facilitators worked closely with the school counselors, particularly in the area of career planning and information.

PEER FACILITATOR AIDES

A second way of organizing the use of peer facilitators is to develop the guidance-aide (assistant) program in the counseling center. Some school counselors, for example, have identified students whom they believe can be of assistance in the guidance office. With peer facilitator training, these aides can do much more than the traditional tasks of delivering messages, answering the phone and alphabetizing materials.

For instance, students who are working as aides or assistants might be given a series of training sessions before or after school. Some sessions might even take place during the lunch hour. Regardless, the students could work together on some of the skills and activities described in *Caring and Sharing* and then do additional reading on their own. With this preparation, they could then be more effective (i.e. guiding students to occupational information files, helping new students to feel comfortable in their new environment, assisting the counselor during presentations and co-leading some group guidance and counseling activities).

PEER FACILITATOR CLASSES

The third approach to implementing a peer facilitator program is to form a class. The class could meet for the same amount of time as all other classes on campus and academic credit could be given for successful completion of the program. A peer facilitator class might last one semester or perhaps a full year. (See Chapter XI for a possible curriculum calendar). The ideas and activities presented in *Caring and Sharing* could serve as the class curriculum.

Obviously, this approach requires more organization and a specified director or trainer who will teach the class. The person might be designated as "Program Director." While this person could be a teacher on the faculty, the most likely candidate will be one of the school counselors because the person should have had preparation and training in basic counseling skills. Counselors usually have the necessary flexibility to organize and work with most of the student body and faculty. Still another option is to have a counselor and teacher work together as "co-directors." In this case they could share teaching and supervisory responsibilities. They could also draw upon the special resources that each has to offer and provide the kind of mutual support that is helpful.

CHOOSING THE TRAINING MODEL

Perhaps the most important considerations when choosing a training format for peer facilitators are whether or not the person who is to be the trainer is interested in developing a systematic program and whether or not that person possesses the necessary qualities described in Chapter XV.

Even though peer facilitators can be trained through clubs and guidance aide programs, there are several advantages to organizing the training program along the lines of a class format and offering it as part of the school curriculum. Among these are:

(1) *The program receives more credibility and visibility.*

(2) *Class credit enables the trainer to demand more competence, require more field experiences and provides a viable reward for extensive service by the students.*

(3) *Greater group cohesiveness and an espirit de corps can develop when students meet regularly as part of an organized class.*

(4) *Training is less fragmented and has more continuity.*

(5) *Training is more detailed and there are more opportunities for students to learn experientially and to practice the skills and activities.*

(6) *Classes usually involve more students than other formats and thus more students benefit.*

BUILDING A SUPPORT BASE

The idea of training students to reach out and to work with other students can be both threatening and confusing to many people. It is important to begin by developing a basic support system. You might want to ask the question: "Who in this school/community has the influence and power to help me get this program accepted and started?"

There are at least five main sources of influence in most schools: (1) the school administration, (2) the parents, (3) the school faculty, (4) the student body and (5) certain community interest groups. Deciding which group(s) to approach first can be a critical decision as to the future of your program. Let's look at each of these in more detail.

THE SCHOOL ADMINISTRATION

In many school systems, the principal is the ultimate decision-maker. Most principals will see that the educational environment would be enhanced by having a peer program. Their support is critical. In determining what approach will prove to be the most successful in achieving your goal of administrative approval, you might ask yourself the following questions:

(1) *How would a peer faciilitator program benefit the students? What NEEDS do our students have that could be met through the use of peer facilitators?*

(2) *How would the faculty benefit by having peer facilitators on campus? What faculty pressures could be reduced?*

(3) *What would the administration gain?*

(4) *How much money would the program cost?*

Having answered these questions, consider them now from the perspective of your administrators. Look at the program from their point of view and what they value. Would their answers to these questions be different from yours? What other questions would they ask?

You may want to talk with other people who are also aware of the administration's views and policies and ask for their suggestions. What you perceive as the main reasons for having a peer facilitator program may not be seen by the administration as nearly so important. By analyzing your proposal from their viewpoint, you are increasing the probability that your ideas and suggestions will be considered and given support.

THE PARENTS

Perhaps one of the most overlooked sources of influence in any school community is the parent population. Through the payment of taxes and their votes for members of the school board and state legislators, parents literally "own" the school and thus they have a right to determine what happens at school.

Parents want the best educational opportunities and experiences for their children. They want to know how they can help. Too many times we fail to ask for their support, fearing that parents will not understand and be critical. To the contrary, their contributions can be positive and make a difference.

When seeking the support of parents, ask yourself: "If I were a parent of a student attending this school, what would be of utmost concern to me?" By becoming aware of what is valued, as well as what concerns parents, you can then make a more effective presentation concerning the importance of a peer facilitator program. No doubt you will want to show how the program is related to helping students.

You may want to begin by approaching the most influential parents in the community or you may choose to recruit a more "grass-roots" group of parents. Whatever the approach, it is important that you:

(1) Make a brief presentation about peer influence and its potential for positive impact.

(2) Tell them about your objectives, relating them to learning effectiveness and how the program can help improve the learning climate in the school.

(3) Choose your words carefully and be realistic in your expectations while letting your enthusiasm show.

(4) Give them an opportunity to ask questions, answering them by relating your ideas to their concerns and needs. Be aware of feelings and use high facilitative responses in the discussion. Don't become defensive.

(5) Summarize the themes or significant ideas that have emerged from the discussion/question -and- answer period and again relate these to your plans for the program.

(6) Keep them informed of your progress, especially those parents who show a positive response. This is the beginning of your "ongoing support system."

You may want to start the program and then inform parents of your initial efforts. Or you may want to send parents a letter and invite them to an introductory meeting where you can solicit support for your ideas. For example, in one school with an enrollment of 1500 students, a letter was sent to parents (see Figure 10.1). Approximately 65 parents attended an introductory meeting. Regardless of the numbers who attended, this invitation provided a starting point. Parents were informed and given an opportunity to be involved. In addition to a letter, there may be other forms of announcing the meeting, such as the school newspaper, radio and television stations, local newspapers and so forth.

Finally, involve students in your presentations. Those who are eager and interested in being a part of a program can be most helpful in providing information that shows a need for the program.

Figure 10.1

MEMORANDUM TO PARENTS

To: Parents of Students at Buchholz High School

From: Tom Erney, Peer Facilitator Program Director

You are invited to attend a special meeting for parents on Thursday, May _____, in _____(place)_____, at _____(time)_____. At that time we will talk with you about a new and exciting concept that has the potential for making a positive impact on students at our school and in the district. It involves teaching students to help other students.

We are beginning a peer facilitator program, one that encourages positive peer interactions and focuses on communication skills and decision-making. This kind of program has proven successful in other schools and we want to develop one here. We are enthusiastic about its potential and would like to explore our ideas with you. We value your participation and support and look forward to meeting with you.

If you have any questions, please call the guidance office.

THE FACULTY

Among every school faculty there are teachers who will be excited about peer facilitators and who will promote the program with the rest of the faculty. Their support and cooperation will be much stronger if you can get them personally involved. You may want them to share ideas with the peer facilitator class or ask them how to best use the facilitators around the school. The facilitators might work with some teachers by conducting communication labs in their classes (*Caring and Sharing*, page 181). Teacher opinions and contributions can play an important part in developing your program.

Some teachers, who have had peer facilitators as members of their regular classes, have reported that these students influenced the atmosphere of their classes. Their increased self-confidence and ability to interact with others contributed to more lively class discussions, more penetrating and searching questions, as well as to a more accepting climate. Students encouraged other students to talk and they were better listeners. In brief, they provided a kind of leadership that set the tone for effective learning.

In addition, some teachers have expressed concern about students who are having problems adjusting to class. In one instance, a teacher was working with a class in which two of the students tended to be disruptive. Because there were students in the class who were also part of the peer facilitator program, the matter did not require "disciplinary action." Rather, the peer facilitators confronted the two disruptive students.

Also, because peer facilitators can be a source of tutoring for students who need special attention, they can remove some of the pressure from teachers who feel pushed to meet the many demands and needs of students. High student-teacher ratios are common in most schools and often prevent teachers from giving as much individual attention as they would like. When teachers are made aware of what peer facilitators can do and how they can positively affect the other classrooms, then the faculty is eager to work cooperatively with the trainer and to encourage the development of the program.

THE STUDENT BODY

Student support has played an important part in the beginning stages of many peer facilitator programs. In one school, three seniors,who expressed their concern about the self-destructive behaviors of fellow students who were abusing drugs, provided much of the impetus for getting a program started.

By involving students from the very beginning, the stage is set for establishing credibility and acceptance by the rest of the student body. Student input can increase the probability that your efforts will be seen as "legitimate."

Some attention needs to be given in choosing students who will help plan and implement the program. While the people involved in student government and other leadership positions may be seen by most adults as "the leaders," it should be remembered that the facilitators work with many students, some of whom have little or no respect for recognized student leaders.

Try to include at least one or two students who will represent and speak for the different segments of your school community. Considerable attention will be given to the selection process in Chapter XI.

COMMUNITY INTEREST GROUPS

You may want to get the support and involvement of various community groups when first implementing your program. There are many groups concerned with mental health (e.g., the Junior League, the League of Women Voters, local child abuse councils, the community mental health center, local church alliances), all of whom are potential sources of assistance and support. For example, in several cities the mental health centers have sponsored the formation of peer programs and their staff serves as consultants and trainers for the programs.

MOBILIZING SUPPORT FOR ACTION

Support systems become more essential when attempting to expand the scope of the program. Thus, as a program becomes larger and more involved in community work, you will need to be especially aware of your sources of support.

A trainer may develop an outstanding program on paper and students may be eager to be involved, but without some attention to building a support base, a program might sparkle for a short time and then flicker out. On the other hand, when a strong support base is established, a trainer can move with more confidence, visibility increases and resources multiply. When problems arise, there are more people concerned and willing to help. Building a support base is part of a good public relations program too. Because a good public relations program is essential for a program's success, additional guidelines and suggestions will be presented in Chapter XIII.

Keep in mind that the peer facilitation concept is an organized extention of what is taking place on school campuses every minute of every day. Young people constantly turn to each other for assistance and support. Peer facilitator programs can improve and expand upon the quality of available assistance so that more young people may profit from the nourishment and support of their peers. So, let's get started!

Chapter XI

here's what you need -a checklist

Sometimes it is difficult to know exactly where to start. It can be helpful if you develop a checklist which contains some important items that need early attention. Here are some items that you will probably want to include:

☑ MEETING PLACE

In the ideal situation, you will have a "Peer Facilitator Room." This room would be used exclusively for those activities directly related to the program. First, this prevents schedule conflicts with other teachers and school activities. It enables the trainer and students to use the room throughout the day for special meetings, tutoring, small group sessions and counseling activities. It is your "living space"—a room which is clearly identified for peer facilitators and their work.

In addition, this private room enables you to make use of all the available space and to comfortably arrange the area. Most important, it enables the class to "personalize" the room by decorating it and emphasizing on-going activities. For example, one class decided to make bulletin boards that allowed students to write statements and responses to such unfinished sentences as: "What I fear most about life is. . ." and "What I need most is. . . ." Still other corners of the room reflected the work of the peer facilitators (e.g. photographs that they had taken, letters that had been written and received, newspaper clippings, articles and relevant news items, favorite posters, drawings and pictures).

A carpeted floor or a large rug can be useful because it helps create an informal and relaxed atmosphere, as well as provide a more comfortable setting when students sit on the floor. It also reduces the noise level. Bean bag chairs, large sofa pillows and other comfortable furniture can help set the tone for a more personalized setting and provide more opportunities for different kinds of room arrangements, especially those where students work together in small groups. The activities suggested in this book and in *Caring and Sharing* require some flexible space. For example, a class of 25 will frequently work in small groups of five or six. While traditional school furniture can still be used, the emphasis upon flexible and comfortable furnishings not only creates a relaxed working environment, but it can expedite the movement of students from large to small groups and vice versa.

If this type of room is not feasible, then a second option is to "share" a classroom with another teacher. It may be someone who has a planning period during your scheduled class time. This often limits the amount of personalizing that you can do to the room, but it can still be arranged comfortably.

If no classroom is available, a third possibility is to meet with the peer facilitators in the guidance office or some other non-instructional setting. The size and location of the meeting place usually determines the number of students that can participate in any one class meeting.

One important consideration in selecting a meeting place is the amount of available privacy. Training sessions seem to go smoothly when there are a minimum number of visual and auditory distractions. Also, some students receiving tutoring and/or participating in a small group led by facilitators prefer as much privacy as possible.

☑ MEETING TIMES

The most desirable and convenient time for peer facilitators to meet is during a regularly scheduled class period. This insures that the facilitators are available for training and projects and that they are not committed to other activities. It provides you with the most flexibility and assures continuity.

However, if a class period is not feasible, facilitators can meet during the lunch hour, after school or even on the weekend. It is possible, for example, to have most of the initial training phase held as part of a weekend retreat(s). Then, the field experiences or projects could take place during the school day. Or it may be possible to arrange a combination of during and after school training hours.

One trainer began with lunch hour meetings (two times a week for three weeks). After interest picked up, a Saturday workshop was planned. This one full day of activities and skills practice enabled the facilitators to talk about matters in more detail and to explore concepts without interruption. They ended the experience with a "pot luck" dinner, which added to the group's cohesiveness and commitment.

☑ SELECTION PROCESS

WHO WILL BE SELECTED?

This is one of the most important decisions that a trainer makes. Helping other people to make the most of their lives is serious business and calls for those involved to assume an exceptional amount of responsibility and caring. The program is not suited for those who behave irresponsibly or who require constant supervision. While there is no magic formula which guarantees results, the following ideas have proven helpful.

The selection factors can vary somewhat between beginning and established programs. Two of the major differences are: (1) in a beginning program there are no "current" peer facilitators to help in the screening and (2) the credibility of the program has not yet been established.

Students selected as part of the first group of peer facilitators will help build a foundation for future groups. Most new programs are viewed carefully and analytically. Thus, in the beginning you may want to select students who will be immediately involved and care about the progress of the program.

For example, one trainer decided to begin a program by selecting students who he thought would be interested in such work and who would be responsive to the demands of the program. He selected students who were well-known throughout the school and, for the most part, were accepted favorably by other students. Moreover, his first group was made up of achievers and the "extra" work of being a peer facilitator did not detract from their academic studies.

Both faculty and parents recognized the students as outstanding and believed that they would make excellent models for others. These students learned quickly and were verbally skilled. They were already at ease in their interpersonal relationships with others. The trainer also felt comfortable and relaxed with these students and it was easy to form a cohesive group. Consequently, they accomplished many objectives and eventually brought a lot of positive recognition to the program.

This same trainer also realized that some students in the student body were not responsive to the help of this group because they did not identify with them. The facilitators were viewed as the "elite" and "favorites" by some who, interesting enough, often needed the most help. Therefore, it required special efforts and encouragement before they learned to "reach out" to those who were not part of their "in group."

Later, after some experience, the trainer decided to include some other students in the class who were less visible as "leaders," but who had the potential for facilitating those labeled "difficult to reach." Still later, when another selection process was started, the trainer decided to identify and include a few students who were a part of the more difficult factions in the student body. These students proved to be as successful in their efforts as those who entered the program with recognized leadership credentials. Training, therefore, became treatment.

If you are just beginning a program, you may want to select a few students with whom *you* would like to work. As you gain more experience and confidence and as the program becomes more established, you can then expand its scope and perhaps include students who represent the many factions of the school and community.

HOW MANY SHOULD BE SELECTED?

This is a difficult question to answer. It will often depend upon the commitment, energy level, time demands, skills and objectives of the trainer. The number can also be influenced by the space that is available for training and the kinds of projects that are viewed as part of the "field experiences."

There is no doubt that every student body can benefit from having a large number of students involved in peer facilitator training. It simply means that there will be more sensitive and responsive young people on the campus. Practically speaking, however, there is a limit to the number of students who can work with one trainer and a specific program. Ultimately, the number of participating students must be a reflection of the trainer's skills and the objectives of the program.

As a general rule, one class or club might be limited to a maximum of 25 students. This number can work conveniently in groups of five or six and feasibly use the space in a classroom. Beginning trainers might find it easier to limit the number even more. Perhaps twelve or fifteen is more manageable and some will want to start with as few as six. If the group is too small, they lose the benefit of sharing experiences with others and the impact of some of the training activities. If the group is too large, then the trainer—unless assisted by veteran peer facilitators who are repeating the program—cannot give the individual attention that is needed to help students develop their competencies.

Finally, the number might also be influenced by the kind of "field experiences" or projects that have been identified for the class or club. If projects are limited in terms of involvement— such as one or two structured interviews, or perhaps four or five structured group experiences—then the number of participating facilitators can be increased. On the other hand, when projects are more varied and the skills required are more extensive, then it seems practical to work with a smaller group.

HOW CAN STUDENTS BE RECRUITED?

One way to help identify and recruit students to be in a peer facilitator program is to ask for recommendations from faculty members and administrators. Asking for their input is also an involvement process. It can create more support. For instance, you might ask them to nominate students for the program and to rate those students on the following criteria:

(1) Concern for the welfare of others

(2) Ability to listen and to understand others

(3) Flexibility—ability to adjust to new situations

(4) Self-confidence

(5) Dependability—responsible and able to follow through with assigned tasks

(6) Honesty

(7) Potential for leadership

After receiving the nominations and ratings, you could then make your selection. Or you might prefer to meet with those nominated, explain your program and ideas and survey the interest of those present. They might rate themselves on the same criteria. Some trainers prefer to interview students individually before making a final decision.

Another approach is to make the selection process more open by announcing to the student body that a peer facilitator program will be offered and that those interested should attend an orientation meeting. An article might be written about the objectives of the program in the school newspaper. Some students might be encouraged to make announcements in their classes or clubs. When students attend the open meeting, their interests and time commitments can be surveyed and they can rate themselves on the selection criteria. This self-referral process often leads to the discovery of some outstanding peer facilitators who are highly motivated and committed. Sometimes these same persons have been inadvertently overlooked by other referral sources.

Another interesting approach that has proven most successful with an established peer facilitator program has been the use of veteran peer facilitators as "screeners." These students usually have the necessary experience, knowledge, sensitivity and skill to help select students who will be most responsive to the training and successful in their work.

More specifically, here are ten steps that have been followed when peer facilitators were used as part of the screening process:

(1) Appropriate announcements are made and opportunities for learning more about the program are arranged. In some cases, current peer facilitators (screeners) conduct open noon hour meetings in which they answer questions about the program. The film, *Peer Facilitators: Youth Helping Youth*, is shown to illustrate the nature of the class, its activities and some of the field experiences.

(2) A sign-up list is then posted in the guidance office. Students who have attended the open noon hour meetings and who are further interested in becoming peer facilitators then sign their name and, thus, express a desire to take part in the formal screening process.

(3) The trainer then sends invitations to those who signed the list, asking them to attend a screening session. These sessions are arranged at different times over a period of about 1-2 weeks and involve about 6-8 students at one time.

(4) Each screening session is arranged for about 50 minutes. During the first five to ten minutes, the trainer and the one or two peer facilitators who are working as helpers or "screeners" are introduced. An outline of the process is presented, which includes time for (a) a self-report form and (b) a group sharing activity. The trainer leaves the room and the peer facilitators act as group leaders.

(5) The self-report form is then administered to the group. This is a rating form and includes the seven criteria mentioned previously (page 128).

(6) After students have completed the form, the peer facilitators conduct a "go-around" in which the members, in turn, share one thing about themselves from their form. After each has spoken, the candidates are encouraged to talk about the experience and their feelings.

(7) During the final few minutes of the session, the trainer returns to the group, answers questions and thanks them for taking part in the process.

(8) After the students leave the session, the peer facilitators rate each student form 1-10, with 1 being high, and write a brief rationale for each rating.

(9) Three ratings (self, screener and one by the trainer) serve as a pool of information. The final selection is also based on such considerations as (1) sex, (2) race, (3) grade level, (4) social group and (5) potential for establishing a working relationship with the trainer. Obviously, a class that is composed of all one "type of student" (e.g. all girls, all athletes, all whites), is limited in its potential to learn from each other and to be of service to others.

(10) After students have been selected, appropriate announcements are then sent to each student who signed up (see Figures 11.1 and 11.2).

Figure 11.1

ACCEPTANCE NOTICE

May 26, 19___

Congratulations! It is my pleasure to inform you that you have been selected to be a peer facilitator next year. It is going to be an exciting time. . . one of the most rewarding experiences you'll ever have. Have a good summer and come prepared in the fall to get involved in the challenging movement of "youth helping youth."

Sincerely,

Tom Erney, Director
Peer Facilitator Program

Figure 11.2

REJECTION NOTICE

May 26, 19___

It is very difficult for me to report that you will not be a part of the Peer Facilitator Program next year.

Only 20 students out of approximately 85 applications could participate. A number of factors were involved in making a final decision. Almost everyone who was screened would have done well in the program, but it is impossible to work with a large group.

If you want to discuss this decision, please contact me in the guidance office.

Sincerely,

Tom Erney, Director
Peer Facilitator Program

This more detailed selection process was developed for an established program in which it is common for at least 75-100 students to participate in the screening process. Unfortunately, only 20 *new* positions have been available each year (five students repeat as veteran facilitators). Thus, it is important to be fair, open and show respect.

When there are only a few positions available because of trainer limitations, and when there are many who would like to be a part of the program, the selection process becomes even more difficult. It is sometimes a painful experience for the trainer, who must make the final decision.

It is disappointing for those who are not chosen—many of whom would have done well in the program. Ideally, of course, it would be best if all students who indicate an interest and commitment could receive the training. This kind of extensive peer facilitator program, however, is currently beyond the scope of most guidance programs, but it is something worth working toward.

☑ PARENTS' NIGHT

Once the new facilitators are selected, a Parents' Night is desirable. The purpose of this meeting is to inform the parents about the program's objectives and activities and to enlist their support. Both the facilitators and their parents are invited to attend.

Here is a general outline of what might be done at Parents' Night:

(1) Introduction of the trainer. Tell some personal background and how you came to be interested in the program.

(2) Explain the purpose of the meeting. Acquaint parents with the objectives of the program and answer questions.

(3) Outline objectives on board or overhead projector.

(4) Show the film, *Peer Facilitators: Youth Helping Youth.*

(5) Answer more questions.

(6) Have the parents experience one of two brief "training activities."

(7) Ask for their support. Obtain the parent permission and insurance form.

An example of one invitation that was sent to parents is shown in Figure 11.3.

Figure 11.3

PARENTS' NIGHT INVITATION

Hello,

I am writing to invite you to a gathering of parents, students and others associated with the Peer Facilitator Program at Buchholz High School. We are getting together on October 1 at 7:30 p.m. in room 401 to discuss the program, answer any questions you may have and generally fill you in on the rationale and philosophy of the class.

Your child is going to be involved in a significant educational program, one that gives students an opportunity to grow as human beings and to help others.

Please take 1½ hours of your time and be with us. You'll be glad that you did.

Sincerely,

Tom Erney, Director
Director, Peer Facilitator Program

P.S. Please sign and return.

_____Yes, I plan to attend "Parents' Night" on Thursday, October 1.

_____No, I will not be able to attend.

_____

_____
(Parents' signatures)

☑ PARENT PERMISSION

The Peer Facilitator Program is a unique offering, and in most schools, it will be necessary to get parent permission before students can participate in the program's activities. This is especially true when students take part in a field experience that is off-campus, perhaps at a neighboring elementary or middle school. In this case, transportation can become an issue with liability and insurance a concern to both parents and administrators. Therefore, a *Parent Permission Form* (see Figure 11.4) might be in order. You will want to consult with your administration regarding this point. But, keep it simple and avoid using language that may create unnecessary concerns.

Figure 11.4

PARENT PERMISSION FORM

This is to certify that _____
has my permission to participate in the Buchholz Peer Facilitator Program.

I am aware that neither the school nor Mr. Erney will be liable for any injury and/or accident which occurs while my child is involved in any activity related to or sponsored by the Peer Facilitator Program. I also realize that my child may be transported to various schools and agencies in cars driven by other students. In the event of an accident, I will assume full responsibility for my child during this time.

_____
Parent Signature
_____
Date

☑ PROGRAM CALENDAR

Every trainer needs to develop a program calendar. This calendar outlines the activities and projects related to the program. It is the general plan for the training of the peer facilitators and their field experiences. It reflects the overall goals of the trainer and the direction in which the program will move.

Program calendars can be planned around four basic phases:

(1) *The Initial Training Phase.*

(2) *Field Experience Phase.*

(3) *Evaluation, Added Training and Planning Phase.*

(4) *Closure Phase.*

Although some peer facilitator programs will be shorter in duration than others, these same phases will be applicable. Let's look at them in more detail.

THE INITIAL TRAINING PHASE

During this first phase, students develop a sense of belonging to the group in a trusting and accepting atmosphere in which to try new ideas as they self-disclose about themselves. They are introduced to the basic skills of the program: listening, responding, praising, confronting and decision-making. They gain an understanding of the program's objectives, rationale and philosophy. After becoming acquainted with the different peer facilitator roles, they practice related skills. Practice, practice and more practice! They learn by doing.

The duration of this phase, of course, will depend upon the program's objectives and projects. If a program, for example, has limited objectives and intends to enable students to participate in one relatively brief field experience, then this phase might be about 18-20 hours.

On the other hand, if it is part of a year-long program and students are part of a peer facilitator class, then this phase may be as long as 45-50 hours, or approximately nine weeks of school. Regardless, it is the most important phase of the program and will take the most planning and energy.

FIELD EXPERIENCE PHASE

Field experience provides opportunities for peer facilitators to use their knowledge and skills. After the initial training phase, students usually enter a field experience that gives them a chance to be successful in reaching out and facilitating others. For this reason, a popular first field experience for middle and high school students is a project in which they work with elementary school students.

For example, after nine weeks of training, a class of peer facilitators (25) entered three different elementary schools and met with teachers who assigned them different students. These facilitators served as tutors, big brothers/ sisters and group discussion leaders. Each facilitator worked with the host-teacher and planned appropriate activities for the young children. After a period of about nine weeks, this initial field experience was terminated and the peer facilitators shared their experiences in class and then planned another experience.

In still another beginning field experience, some peer facilitators took part in a guidance project and participated as co-leaders of small groups in their own high school. They worked closely with their school counselors, who had divided a large group of students into several smaller groups for discussion purposes. These groups were structured, activities were outlined and the peer facilitators has a clear idea of both the activities and their responsibilities.

Obviously, it is in the best interests of the training, students and the program if the initial experience is a successful one. Therefore, the first field experience will probably be more structured, shorter in duration and more closely supervised. When facilitators experience success, their involvement and commitment increase.

After their first field experience is completed, additional experiences can be initiated. Sometimes these take the form of a "project" which identifies a population, time period, goal and peer intervention strategies.

EVALUATION, ADDED TRAINING AND PLANNING PHASE

Peer facilitators need an opportunity to talk about their work. They should be able to speak about their unpleasant feelings, as well as their pleasant ones. "Processing the experience" is a term that is used to describe how trainers and peer facilitators examine their work. They analyze and explore the events and their feelings. They try to gain some insight. This "open sharing" is one form of evaluation. However, more formal means may also be used. In this case, facilitators might complete a questionnaire or write a paper. The activities outlined in Chapter VII in *Caring and Sharing,* as well as Chapter VII in this book, can be useful.

After looking back on their efforts, the trainer and peer facilitators can then recognize additional areas where they would like more training and information. This occasion is also used for review of the facilitative skills. Role playing is a common activity. This added training component will help the facilitators approach the next field experience with more confidence.

This phase is usually concluded with preparation for the next field experience. Plans are outlined. Peer interventions are discussed. Additional resource people are sometimes invited in as a part of the planning process. The facilitators also practice some of the activities and skills that they plan to use.

This particular phase—evaluation, added training and planning— is repeated after each field experience. It not only provides a type of closure to each experience, but it focuses on the next steps. At the end of the last field experience, however, a more formal closure phase is needed.

CLOSURE PHASE

This is the final moment. It is the time when the peer facilitators and the trainer reflect back upon the program's activities and their personal experiences. More than likely, it will involve some formal evaluation procedures of the program, but it is also an opportunity for self-evaluation. Peer facilitator programs, especially those that have followed the general principles outlined in this book, provide students a powerful personal experience. It is one that they want to talk about and the final meetings of the program deserve some moments of recognition and celebration. It is frequently an opportune time for the peer facilitators to focus on what the program has meant to them. What are their plans now? What else do they want to have happen in their lives? How do they plan to make those things happen?

You may want to make time for a final feedback experience, one in which students in the class give and receive feedback. Even though the students will probably see each other on campus, in other classes and at other school events, the final session is an excellent time for "One Final Statement. . . ." Sometimes, it is a final *"Strength Bombardment."* Each student needs and deserves that final moment of positive words from the others. No doubt, as a trainer, you will want to plan for and participate in these special activities and moments in the final stages of your program.

☑ CURRICULUM CALENDAR

After you have developed a program calendar, you will want to turn your attention to a "curriculum calendar," which outlines the daily events of the training phase. It is the "lesson plan" for teaching students the basic knowledge and skills that will be needed prior to their entering the first field experience.

This calendar will also vary according to program structure and objectives. But, there are a few fundamental concepts and skills that are a part of most peer facilitator programs.

This book and *Caring and Sharing* were designed to help trainers and peer facilitators develop a workable and appropriate training program. They focus upon basic concepts and activities. If you are designing a peer facilitator class, you may want to plan a 45-50 hour training phase. Thus, it is possible to have the students read and discuss the concepts in each of the chapters of *Caring and Sharing*, with perhaps five hours or one week devoted to each chapter.

The three activities presented in *Caring and Sharing,* plus the additional two activities presented in this book, provide you with a selection that will help you teach concepts and skills. Assign those that you believe fit your objectives and programs. Choose those that apply to your goals and that you enjoy doing. Add others that you have discovered. Modify any or all to meet your needs.

If you are forming a peer facilitator club or training guidance aides, your training curriculum will be more limited and you will need to be more selective. However, you will probably want to focus on Chapters III, IV, V and VI in *Caring and Sharing*. The training principles discussed in this book will still apply.

☑ CODE OF ETHICS

There is no official code of ethics for peer facilitators. However, people in the different helping professions have developed ethical principles and they are applicable to helpers at all levels. You may want to review the code of ethics suggested for school counselors or the ethical standards published by the American Personnel and Guidance Association (1961). Perhaps after some review, you might want to discuss the matter with your facilitators and have them develop their own code.

☑ ETC., ETC., ETC. . . .

As a trainer of peer facilitators, you will want to develop a program that meets both your needs and the needs of your students. You must be the final judge of what works best. Develop a checklist of "things to do," one that will help you get organized. This list must be relevant to your own school and situation. However, here are a few more items that might be worth considering:

_____*Inventory the related resources in and around school.*

_____*Order resource materials (books, posters, reference materials, educational kits, films and so forth).*

_____*Develop supplementary handouts and forms.*

_____*Contact guest speakers.*

_____*Make a list of possible field experiences.*

_____*Talk with the school librarians about tutoring materials.*

_____*Make a list of needed media equipment (tape recorders, record players and film projectors).*

_____*Develop a filing system for new ideas, as well as a record of events—personal log, lesson plans. This can be invaluable for future reference.*

_____*Arrange transportation, if needed.*

_____*Consider legal forms, if needed.*

Chapter XII

field experiences for peer facilitators

After the initial training phase, peer facilitators will be ready to try their new skills outside the classroom in a "field experience." *Field experience refers to a setting, or project in a setting, in which peer facilitators work for an extended period of time.* It requires the facilitators to work in one of the three roles—tutor, big brother/sister, group discussion leader—or a variation of these roles.

MOVING INTO THE FIELD

There are many places where peer facilitators can be helpful. The most obvious, of course, is the immediate school setting. However, peer facilitators can also be very effective in other places (e.g. hospitals, retirement homes, convalescent centers, juvenile shelters and so on). The list of possibilities is endless and potential learning experiences are abundant.

Regardless of the setting, most people will need to know what peer facilitators can do. Is it worth the time and energy to work with them? Will the experience create more problems than solutions? Can they really be "facilitative?" People will want to know more about your program and you will want to tell them.

It is most important to have a well-organized, clear and concise statement of your objectives. No matter if you are meeting with a school principal, a group of teachers or the director of an agency, the manner and clarity with which you present your case will greatly affect their attitudes and willingness to cooperate. Plan ahead.

One effective way of explaining what peer facilitators are and what they can do is to show the film, *Peer Facilitators: Youth Helping Youth.* The film may not tell everything that you are planning to do, but it can help illustrate general objectives and methods. This twenty-six-minute film is "worth a thousand words" and has proven to have a positive impact on others. It can also be worked into a question/answer session, during which more specific concerns can be discussed.

If your program has been in operation for a while, you may have some pictures that can be used in a slide-tape presentation. Or you may want to make a video tape that shows facilitators in action. All of these methods and others will help you "sell" your ideas and generate enthusiasm for the program.

It is also helpful when peer facilitators accompany the trainer and take part in a public presentation where you are providing information. Their honest reactions, genuine excitement and interest usually adds an extra dimension that cannot be presented in any other way. Students can communicate the concept to others better than most adults because the program is about and for them.

LAYING THE GROUNDWORK

When field experiences are being developed, it is important to consider who will be the "host." This person is someone in the setting who coordinates and helps supervise peer facilitators. For example, if facilitators are assigned to work in the high school guidance office, then one of the counselors might be a host. This counselor, then, would be responsible for orienting them to the setting, as well as helping them identify specific tasks and projects they might do. Or if facilitators are assigned to an elementary school, teachers might serve as hosts. They could introduce them to their classes and help them develop a schedule of tasks and activities.

In some cases there could be a liaison-person or "co-host." For instance, school counselors are valuable coordinators and they can introduce the concepts to teachers, identify appropriate classroom settings and help supervise. Let them work directly with the teachers. If a school does not have a counselor, then perhaps one teacher might be identified as the designated host who will coordinate efforts. The host usually has a better understanding of the setting and can help structure a positive experience for the facilitators.

Working with hosts is an important part of your role as trainer. They can help you determine how much training is necessary before a project can be started. They can identify special opportunities. Without effective, caring and interested hosts, field experiences can be frustrating and unproductive. Therefore, it is important to sell hosts on the program and to get them involved in developing appropriate field experiences. Hosts will want to know about their role and your expectations.

Here are some suggestions that were provided to a group of elementary school hosts:

(1) Acquaint the facilitators with the setting. Give them a tour and help them feel comfortable.

(2) Introduce them to those with whom they will be working and other appropriate resource persons.

(3) Help them learn names.

(4) Tell them where you might be in case of emergencies.

(5) Let your attitude of trust and confidence show—it's contagious.

(6) Start slowly and then add more responsibilities as they become more relaxed, experienced and confident.

(7) Tell them about any specific rules or policies that are related directly to their work.

(8) Be available to help them explore successes and problems.

(9) If a problem is developing, don't let it build up. Contact the trainer early.

(10) Don't forget these facilitators are "volunteering" their time and want to feel appreciated!

WORKING IN THE SCHOOLS

As you are talking with the host or contact person, you will also be working toward some specific kinds of experiences and clarifying how the facilitators can be of particular help. You can identify tasks and projects by obtaining referrals from teachers and administrators.

OBTAINING REFERRALS

One form that was used to obtain referrals is shown in Figure 12.1. This form was used with elementary school teachers after they had attended a faculty meeting where the general nature of the peer facilitator program was described. The form was distributed to all teachers and they were given a few days to think about the needs of their own students and how a peer facilitator might work with them.

Those who desired the services of a facilitator returned the form to the elementary school counselor, who reviewed the requests and made recommendations to the trainer. The trainer, counselor and teachers then worked together to match students with students, considering such criteria as sex, race, special interests, hobbies goals and facilitator skills.

Figure 12.1

PEER FACILITATOR REQUEST FORM

To: Counselors and Administrators

From: Tom Erney

We are ready to begin another year in which peer facilitators from Buchholz High School will volunteer to work in the elementary schools of Alachua County. Hundreds of elementary students have received some very special attention and caring due to our program. This year we have twenty-five juniors and seniors who are receiving training in interpersonal relationships. These students are being trained to fulfill the following roles:

Figure 12.1

(continued)

(1) GROUP DISCUSSION LEADER—Works with 3-6 students in a small group. The primary focus is upon developing the affective domain of the child, plus listening and social skills. Approaches include use of the DUSO kit, Magic Circles and Values Clarification activities.

(2) BIG BROTHER/SISTER—Gives individual attention for those elementary students who need a more focused and involved relationship. This has been the most requested role at the elementary level.

(3) TUTOR—Helps students who are in need of academic assistance. Our experiences (and research) suggest that the personal relationship is an important part in the development of academic skills.

Please Note: Peer facilitators generally come to the elementary schools on Mondays, Wednesdays and Fridays. In general, the hours have to be between 11:00 a.m. and 12:20 p.m. We can negotiate other times, if needed.

If you would like to have a peer facilitator work with one or more of your students, please fill in the request form below.

Teachers Name _____

School _____

Grade Level _____

Role(s) Requested _____

How can the peer facilitator be of assistance? _____

_____

Name of Student _____ Sex _____

Special Interests of the Student _____

_____

Are there any special considerations to think about when assigning a peer to this student? _____

_____

Another approach to obtaining referrals is shown in Figure 12.2. A memo to counselors and administrators identified peer facilitators who could be helpful in orienting new students to the school. This simple approach of announcing the availability of facilitators might be modified for other situations. It also gives visibility to the program.

OFFERING SPECIAL SERVICES

Classroom Guidance

Sometimes a particular service or project can be offered to teachers. For example, some social studies and English teachers, upon learning about Communications Labs (*Caring and Sharing,* page 181), worked with a trainer to develop a series of classroom guidance experiences related to their curriculum. The use of peer facilitators enabled the teachers to work more with small groups and to have more productive discussions. There was increased class involvement and, consequently, more excitement. Learning was enhanced.

After a program has been established and after it has gained visibility and credibility, teachers and administrators frequently suggest interesting ideas. They offer creative suggestions as they learn what peer facilitators can do to enhance the learning of others and help them in their work. They become even more willing to free students to participate in various activities and projects.

Test Interpretation

In one instance, peer facilitators were used to help other students talk about the results of the *Differential Aptitude Test (DAT)*. A series of meetings were arranged by the school counselors, who were responsible for administering and interpreting the results. Peer facilitators were used to help students become more involved with their test results through small discussion groups.

Figure 12.2

MEMORANDUM ANNOUNCING SERVICES

TO: Counselors and Administrators

FROM: Tom Erney

The following Peer Facilitators are willing to have a *new student* spend the day with them:

SENIORS

Pam Walton
Trish Heller
Luann Langham
Anna Matell
Scott Kilgore
Pattie Pace
Sallie Winter
David Smith
Susan Myrick
Bill Benck
Nick Wise
Robyn Wagemaker
Mary Beth Farmer
Janet Griffin

JUNIORS

Marte Vanderwerf
Dean White
Darryl Blanford
Richard Anderson

Note: Please contact the facilitators when their services are desired. Be sure to check and see if they are "relatively free" on the day they are to help.

These facilitators enabled the counselors to make the best use of their time and, together, they reached 550 students in two days. Initial presentations were made by the counselors to groups of about thirty students each. This larger group was then divided into smaller units of about five or six students.

Peer facilitators were given specific training related to leading or co-leading the small groups in discussion. Counselors moved among the groups, supervising and consulting. It was a "personalized" approach to test interpretation. More students had an opportunity to talk about their test results with someone and it increased their meaning.

In contrast, a similar high school was entirely dependent upon counselors alone. They also met with students in large and small groups, but it took approximately three to four weeks longer and the project dominated their daily schedule.

It was necessary to request the services of facilitators and to obtain permission from their teachers to miss class. Facilitators were excused to participate in the project, unless it detracted from their academic progress. A request form for that particular experience is shown in Figure 12.3.

Figure 12.3

DAT EXPLANATION

To the Teachers of _____

From: Gayle, Gussie and Tom (counselors)

In the fall of this school year, we administered the *Differential Aptitute Test (DAT)* to all tenth grade students. At this time, the tenth graders also completed a detailed *Career Planning Questionnaire*. The results of these two instruments have been sent to us. We are making plans to interpret the results.

We have decided that a very personal, small group explanation of the results would be most beneficial in terms of realistic career planning, as well as more accurate course selection. We need the assistance of students in the Peer Facilitator Program.

We are requesting that the above-named peer facilitator be permitted to miss your class on April 26 and 27 in order to assist us. The peer facilitators realize that they are responsible for all class work and assignments. If you feel that this student should *not* be excused on the designated days, then write this on the form. Otherwise, your signature will indicate that you have granted permission for this person to work with us on the 26th and 27th.

If you have any questions, please contact us.

1st_____

2nd_____

3rd_____

4th_____

5th_____

6th_____

Vocational Exploration Groups

Sometimes a project can take place in either the guidance office or the classroom. For example, in the state of Georgia, peer facilitators are experimenting with a program called the *Vocational Exploration Group (VEG)*. This is a small group experience for about five to six participants (Daane, 1972). They learn about the world of work through activities, which include a focus on job entry and function, job satisfiers, interests and skills.

Students talk about jobs they would like to have and those that they would not like to have. They get feedback from others in the group and, eventually, arrive at a "next step." Before leaving the group, each member decides upon a next step to take within two weeks— something that will help the person move toward a career goal or get more information about it.

The *VEG* is a packaged program that contains job information books, visual aides, writing materials, job inventories and a leader book. It is the leader book that has attracted most attention because it outlines in detail the sequential tasks and procedures to be followed.

In addition, the leader statements are printed in bold type so that the *VEG* leader may read the procedures and then lead the group in the activity. Because the group is structured, it has a great deal of potential as a project for peer facilitators . It has been used with success at both the middle and senior high school level.

In-school Suspensions

Discipline is a problem in most schools. What do students do when they think that they are being treated unfairly and do not want to work with a teacher? Sometimes student-teacher differences lead to untimely conflicts and troublesome confrontations, which may result in student suspension.

When students are suspended and prevented from coming to school, they are no longer available for help from school personnel and they frequently present problems to the community. Parents also object strongly when their child is denied admission to the campus. In-school suspension has become another alternative and peer facilitators can play an important role in this approach.

In this case students with problems are assigned to a "Time-Out" room within the school. It is a "cooling down" place where students may continue their studies without having to immediately settle their problems with a teacher. This time is often productive if the suspended student has an opportunity to think about the situation and discuss it with someone, perhaps a counselor or peer facilitator. After some time has passed and after an agreement between student and teacher has been reached, the student then returns to the class.

More often than not, in-school suspension results from a breakdown in student-teacher relations and communication. With the help of counselors and peer facilitators, many students can remain in school and resolve their problems with others.

WORKING IN COMMUNITY AGENCIES

There is plenty to do in school settings. Many successful peer facilitator programs have confined their projects or field experiences to their own school. Some high schools have expanded their efforts to include elementary and middle schools, but always working in the context of a school setting. More recently, some trainers have found that they can add an extra ingredient to their program by working with community agencies.

First, there are many young people who are not attending school and who can benefit from meeting with a peer facilitator. For example, there are some students who are confined to a hospital bed for long periods of time. It can be lonely for them. They miss the interaction with peers that comes when attending school. Because of their illness or injury, some get behind in their academic studies and this only adds to their problems. A peer facilitator can be a liaison between the school and student. In addition, the facilitator can provide the hospitalized student with the kind of timely personal support that is frequently needed.

In one instance a young boy was retained in a juvenile shelter. The family situation complicated matters. During this critical period, a peer facilitator "reached out" to the boy and provided him a supportive relationship and encouragement. The facilitator visited the boy at the shelter. "We talked, played games and talked some more." The case worker, with whom this experience was coordinated and who acted as host, reported that the timely visits by the facilitator lessened the boy's feelings of rejection and isolation.

In addition, *peer facilitators can also work with adults.* In this case, the term "peer facilitator" should not be taken literally. Rather, the emphasis is upon being a "facilitator" and providing a helping relationship. There are many older citizens, for example, whose feelings of loneliness and worthlessness result from being isolated from others.

In one situation, Anne, a peer facilitator, visited a retirement center and developed a friendly relationship with a retired teacher. As part of her field experience, she visited Mrs. Howard twice a week and they became friends. They went shopping, visited the local park and sometimes had lunch together. During these times, Anne encouraged the woman to talk about herself and her past experiences. It was a delightful experience for both. Mrs. Howard said: "I really look forward to Anne's visits. She is such a friendly person and I would do anything for her." Later Anne reported: "I really learned a lot about life and the importance of living it to the fullest."

Expanding the field experiences into the community can give your program more visibility and provide more unique learning experiences for the peer facilitators. They quickly learn that their skills can be applied in all aspects of life.

PREPARING THE STUDENTS

No matter how thorough the training program may have been and no matter how skilled the peer facilitators may be, there is always some initial anxiety as they prepare to enter field experiences—especially the first one. They are nervous. They sometimes doubt their abilities and complain: "We need more time." Trainers too have their concerns and moments of anxiety. Having the students practice their skills in class under your watchful eyes is different than sending them to a field experience setting. The secret to most successful programs is planning and approaching matters systematically.

You may want to develop another checklist which will help you to prepare the students for their first field experience. Depending upon your training program and field experiences, the items may differ. However, here are some tasks that you might want to include.

(1) Assign the facilitators to settings. Using a *Peer Facilitator Request Form* (see Figure 12.1), it is possible to match peer facilitators to field experience settings. While the students will want to be involved in any decision, assignments are made by the trainer. More often than not, peers enjoy working together in their first assignments and can be assigned as "co-facilitators" or as a team.

(2) Tell the facilitators about the setting. Students are anxious to get as many details as possible: "Where is it?" "Who's the host?" "Who will I be working with?" "Have you told them about us?" "When do we start?" "Where do we meet?" The more detailed you can be in describing the setting, the easier the transition from the classroom to that setting.

(3) Be aware of facilitators' feelings and concerns. At one point in your preparation, you will probably want to provide some kind of activity in which facilitators can talk about feelings and concerns related to their assignment. One approach, after making assignments, is to divide the class into triads and give each of the groups about 8-10 minutes to talk about their reactions and feelings.

Ask the groups to share some of their ideas aloud to the class and listen for general themes and concerns. It helps to elicit important issues and it will enable you to clarify assignments in a more personal manner. It also sets the stage for a productive discussion of things to consider and prepare for.

(4) Help the facilitators think through their first day. "How do I get there?" "Where do I go?" "Who should I talk to?" "What's the name of the host, again?" "How should I dress?" "What will I be doing?" (See *Caring and Sharing*, Capter VIII).

(5) Help them plan their first one or two sessions. They could outline or anticipate some activities that might take place in their first one or two meetings with students or teachers. This may or may not involve a planned activity, but it will at least give them some kind of "game plan."

(6) Encourage them to keep a "log." Remind them to keep a log of their feelings, ideas and plans. It helps them recall and process experiences in class at a later time. These logs can also be used as one means of providing supervision.

(7) Draw up some appropriate handouts. Sometimes it is useful to have a set of notes that will help the facilitators think about their setting and the work or project in that setting. For example, after some discussion in one class, a handout was developed (Figure 12.4) and distributed. It gave the students a quick review of some important ideas. Later on, these same students also developed a handout for leading small group discussions with middle school students (see Figure 12.5).

(8) Help the facilitators develop some kind of accountablity procedure. Field experiences are the final test of the training curriculum and you will want to develop some interesting and challenging ones. When facilitators have been appropriately organized for a project or field experience, there is less tension, more optimism, less confusion, more commitment, less disappointment and more success. Measuring that sucess (or lack of it) is an important part of accountability. Methods for assessing peer facilitator programs are presented in Chapter XIII.

Figure 12.4

WORKING WITH ELEMENTARY SCHOOL STUDENTS

I. STRUCTURE is important for the elementary student. You need to plan your activities. Be sure to communicate to the student(s) what is expected.

For example, the following outlines how to structure a small group activity:

(a) Sit in a circle.
(b) Talk one at a time.
(c) Raise your hand when you wish to speak.
(d) Listen to what other have to say.
(e) No put-downs or killer statements.

Go over the rules each time you meet until *you* feel they know them.

To learn the rules. . . After you have explained the rules, say:

Who can tell me one rule?
Who can tell me another rule?
Who can tell me three rules?

II. LEARN NAMES AND USE THEM. Young children thrive on *ATTENTION!* Remember to recognize each and every one of them when you see them. Learn their names and *use* their names whenever you are speaking with them.

III. VALIDATE the students whenever possible. You enhance their self-concept so much when you let them know that they are special.

IV. SUGGESTED TIME SPAN FOR GROUPS

1st and 2nd grades   . . . . 15 to 20 minutes
3rd grade   . . . . 20 to 25 minutes
4th and 5th grades   . . . . 25 to 30 minutes

Be aware of the students becoming restless. Remember that their attention span is usually shorter than your own.

V. READING TUTOR EXCERCISE. Have the student tell you a story (fantasy). Write or type the story and then have the student read it to you. Also, they can practice printing and spelling by helping you write the story. As they read and share their thoughts, use high facilitative responses.

Figure 12.4

(continued)

VI. SOME MORE THOUGHTS

(1) It is extremely important that the students know that you *truly care* about them. . . and that your caring isn't conditioned on their being good. You can care for them and still not agree with some of their behaviors.

(2) The word "why" is a threatening, non-productive word. Try using words such as "what. . . when. . . how. . . and so forth."

(3) Focus on feelings first! Are you hearing *pleasant* or *unpleasant* feelings? Rember that: Feelings determine perception determine behavior.

(4) Always respect a person's desire for privacy.

(5) Believe in the power of *love* and *personal recognition.*

(6) We all can learn from *each other*. . . no matter what age we may be.

(7) Whenever possible, use open-ended questions and clarifying responses.

VII. SOME ACTIVITIES

(1) Puppets. . . kids love them.
(2) *IALAC Story.*
(3) Fantasy trips.
(4) DUSO activities.
(5) Reading stories from books. . .
    then discussing them.
(6) Role playing various situations.
(7) The playground.
(8) Magic Circle.
(9) Unfinished sentences.
(10) Twenty Questions.
(11) Coloring.
(12) Go-rounds on special topics.
(13) Making a project together.

REMEMBER

Your purpose is *not* to lead students toward *one* point of view. Rather, it is to help them clarify and understand *their own* points of view, to expose them to alternative ways of seeing the world and to promote the development of personal responsibility through the acquisition of the skill of *decision-making.*

RELAX. . . BE YOURSELF AND HAVE FUN!

YOU ARE LOVABLE AND CAPABLE.

Figure 12.5

SUGGESTIONS FOR GROUP WORK

Some general guidelines. . .

1. Plan! The time you spend preparing an interesting activity will often determine how smoothly your session goes.

2. Model the behaviors you feel wil be most productive for the group. If you illustrate that you care and are interested in the attitudes, feelings and values of the group members, this will increase the potential of this behavior being repeated.

3. Have all the necessary materials when you begin. It's often disruptive to the group atmosphere to search for pencils, paper and other supplies.

4. Give clear directions. Make sure that you know exactly what is called for in the activity and then clearly communicate this to the others in the group. *Repeat* significant sections.

5. State any ground rules you may have and the rationale for them.

6. Enthusiasm is important! If you do not appear interested and excited about what the group is about to experience, then how can you expect them to get involved? The more *energy* you put into the group, the more everyone will get out of it.

7. Keep the group moving. Try to keep the group from dragging and the participants from losing interest. Have some interesting questions to draw upon.

8. Keep the group sitting close together. This helps keep people involved in the discussion rather than drifting off.

9. Get the group members to talk with each other. Keep the focus off of you as much as possible.

10. Use high facilitative responses. This will promote the trust level with the group. . . and in you.

11. Be sensitive to who does and who does not share in the group. People's "body language" can tip you off as to how people are feeling. . . and if they want to share/talk.

12. Closure is important. Ask group members to summarize what has been said. . . what have they learned. . . restate important points.

SOME GROUP ACTIVITIES

The Ideal School	Trust Walks
Fifteen Things I Love to Do	Unfinished Sentences
Rank Ordering	Go-rounds
Secret Pooling	Dear Abby
Trust Falls	IALAC Story

Chapter XIII

accountability: telling and selling others

BEING ACCOUNTABLE

Working with peer facilitators is exciting. It's fun to see them get involved in the helping process and to witness the changes that they experience in themselves. It's rewarding to see how they can positively affect the lives of others. Their work often influences the learning climate in a classroom and is pervasive among the student body.

It's also personally satisfying to know that you have made an important contribution to the school and community by organizing, training and supervising peer facilitators. You are going to receive a lot of favorable comments. People will be enthusiastic about the program. However, what measureable evidence will you have to show others? How can you tell that the program is really making a difference?

There have probably been times in your life when people have told you how pleased they were with something that you did. You enjoyed hearing their remarks and some of them still provide fond memories. Unfortunately, you probably forgot many of the positive statements about your work.

When we try repeating the positive statements received from others, something is usually lost in the transition. We may even think as we attempt to repeat the kind words: "Hey, they don't believe me. They don't want to hear this. I'm bragging and they probably think I'm too ego-involved, unable to be objective and too biased." To the contrary, most people are interested in hearing about successful ideas and programs, but *it is often helpful if they can see something that helps tell the story.* It adds to the excitement, objectivity and usually has more impact. Moreover, when we have something to show, as well as to tell, it can play a significant role in accountability and public relations work.

ASSESSING YOUR PROGRAM

The success of your peer facilitator program will depend on the facilitators' self-concepts; their knowledge of the helping process and the helping relationship; and their use of effective communication skills. In addition to assessing each of these components separately, you may also measure both the process and the outcomes of your program by a variety of techniques and instruments.

SELF-CONCEPTS

Self-appraisal can assist facilitators to be more effective and help them gain more self-confidence. Assessment of self received some attention in *Caring and Sharing* (Chapter VII). Some of the instruments presented in that book can be useful. In addition, you will probably want to develop some other measures and procedures that will encourage the facilitators to examine what they are learning and who they are as helping persons.

KNOWLEDGE OF HELPING CONCEPTS

Knowledge of the helping process and the helping relationship is fundamental to the facilitators' efforts. A test of the basic principles will be appropriate because an understanding of these ideas leads to a rationale for their work and gives them a foundation upon which to build strategies. For example, the short assessment instrument presented in Figure 13.1 was designed to help students review some critical concepts and to help the trainer learn more about the progress that students were making in the program.

Figure 13.1

WHAT HAVE YOU BEEN LEARNING?

The following is intended to be a measure of how well you understand what we have been discussing and experiencing during the past three weeks. Answer each question as completely as possible. Good luck!

1. What are the objectives of our program? What are we trying to accomplish?

2. What three roles can peer facilitators fulfill in an elementary school?

3. Explain "values clarification."

4. Outline the *Continuum of Facilitative Responses* and give two (2) examples of each type of response.

5. Describe the five (5) steps involved in making a decision. Choose one decision that *you* are trying to make right now, state the situation and then use these five steps to outline how you would go about making your decision. You do not have to make a final choice. I am interested in the *process* you use.

6. How are you feeling about the class so far? Share positive and negative feelings with me. Also, I hope that you will make some suggestions as to what *you* feel we need to be doing the next few weeks.

NOTE: Answer these questions on another sheet of paper. Keep this copy of the questions. We *will* be discussing them in class next week.

HAVE A GOOD WEEKEND! CHOOSE WISELY AND MAKE YOUR DAYS WHAT *YOU* WANT THEM TO BE!

COMMUNICATIONS SKILLS

The essence of the program is enabling peer facilitators to use effective communication skills with others. That is what the facilitative model is about. Because the helping relationship centers upon verbal communication, considerable attention is given to how students talk with each other.

It is important to help the facilitators examine their speech patterns and their use of helping skills—high facilitative responses and the facilitative feedback model. In addition, they will be using interesting techniques and activities that they have learned along the way and this too can be a productive area for study.

The *Facilitative Skills Checklist* (*Caring and Sharing*, page 154), can help students focus on the particulars of their work— the process that is occurring. In addition, you can learn more about the effect of the training program upon the peers by direct observation of their work. Sometimes this is best accomplished by observing them closely as they participate in class activities or as they work with you on a project.

At other times it might be appropriate to listen to audio tapes, to read typescripts that they have made from their tape recorded interviews, to watch them on a video tape, to see them in a role-playing situation or to read papers they have written about their work.

In one case a trainer had the students periodically write "reaction papers" such as:

I Gave Feedback to Someone I Cared About

A Time When Listening Proved Rewarding

A Student I Know Who Was "Put Down"

Using High Facilitative Responses With My Parents

The Results of Giving Feedback

Helping Someone to Make a Decision—Things I Did To Help

PEER FACILITATORS EFFECTIVENESS INVENTORY (PFEI).

One measure of peer facilitator effectiveness is shown in Figure 13.2. This instrument was designed to help facilitators assess their work, with attention being given to both the *process* and the *outcomes*.

Figure 13.2

PEER FACILITATOR EFFECTIVENESS INVENTORY (PFEI)

I. Read each of the statements below. Indicate the extent of your agreement or disagreement with each statement by circling the appropriate letters to the right: SA—Strongly Agree; A—Agree; U—Uncertain; D—Disagree; SD—Strongly Disagreee. Please respond to all of the statements.

1. The group sessions with the peer facilitators were interesting.   SA A U D SD

2. Group members listened to each other during our sessions.   SA A U D SD

3. Sometimes I was bored during our sessions.   SA A U D SD

4. Everyone participated and shared their thoughts, ideas and feelings in the group.   SA A U D SD

5. Some of the things we talked about made me feel uncomfortable.   SA A U D SD

6. I felt that the peer facilitators were interested in me.   SA A U D SD

7. Sometimes the peer facilitators "put me down."   SA A U D SD

8. The peer facilitators did not think my thoughts and feelings were important.   SA A U D SD

9. The peer facilitators treated me like a friend.   SA A U D SD

10. The peer facilitators were enthusiastic about what they were doing.   SA A U D SD

11. My experience with the peer facilitators helped change my attitudes about certain things.   SA A U D SD

12. My behavior did not change as a result of my experiences in the group.   SA A U D SD

13. My attitude toward *the use of drugs* has changed because of my experiences with the peer facilitators. (Note: Any other special focus can be used here.)   SA A U D SD

Assessing Process with the PFEI

The first ten items enable respondents (e.g. students who meet with the peer facilitator in groups) to report on the process— the ideas and feelings related to *"what happened in the sessions."*

Item   **Statement**

(1) The group sessions with the peer facilitators were *interesting.*

(2) Group members *listened* to each other during our sessions.

(3) Sometimes I was *bored* during our sessions.

(4) *Everyone participated and shared* their thoughts, ideas and feelings in the group.

(5) Some of the things we talked about made me feel *uncomfortable.*

(6) I felt that the peer facilitators were *interested in me.*

(7) Sometimes the peer facilitators *"put me down."*

(8) The peer facilitators *did not think my thoughts and feelings were important.*

(9) The peer facilitators *treated me like a friend.*

(10) The peer facilitators were *enthusiastic* about what they were doing.

Items 1, 2, 4, 6, 9 and 10 emphasize the aspects of involvement, listening, participation, acceptance, closeness and excitement. The issue of involvement, rejection, comfort and acceptance are a part of items 3, 5, 7 and 8. These latter items are stated in the negative and, if desired, they could be reworded in the positive. Other items might be added. Some could be deleted. This instrument could also be reworded for use in evaluating one-to-one sessions.

As the facilitators examine the "process" that took place, they can identify their behaviors, or the behavior of others, that contributed to the report. It is this searching for "cause and effect" that helps them sharpen their skills and be more effective in future relationships.

Assessing Outcomes with the PFEI

While the process is important, many people are concerned primarily with "outcomes." What was the result of your efforts? Did the process make a difference?

An instrument like the *PFEI* can help answer these questions. They ask the respondent to report on the impact of the experience. In some cases, the respondent is asked directly if behavior outside the group is now different. More specifically, items 11-20 focus on *"what happened as a result of the process."*

Item	Statement

(11) My experience with the peer facilitators helped change my *attitudes* about certain things.

(12) My *behavior* did not change as a result of my experience in the group.

(13) My *attitudes toward the use of drugs* has changed because of my experiences with the peer facilitators.

(14) *School* seems more enjoyable as a result of the group experience.

(15) I would *like* to be a peer facilitator someday.

(16) I would *recommend* a similar experience for others.

(17) I *got to know other students better* as a result of our group.

(18) My *understanding* of others increased.

(19) *Understanding of myself* increased because of the group.

(20) My *behavior changed* as a result of my experiences in the group.

Research Based on the PFEI

The *Peer Facilitator Effectiveness Inventory* (Figure 13.2) was used in one study that involved sixty-six fourth and fifth grade elementary school students. Seventeen peer facilitators, who were in grades 9-12 and who attended a public high school in Florida, worked with the students in small groups. When the study began, they had been in a peer facilitator class for about six months. A summary of the responses by the elementary students is shown in *Table II*.

Table II

RESPONSES BY ELEMENTARY
STUDENTS TO THE PFEI

(N=66)

Item Number★★	Positive (SA + A)		Undecided (U)		Negative (D + SD)	
	Frequency	%	Frequency	%	Frequency	%
1	63	95.5	3	4.5	0	0.0
2	53	80.3	4	6.1	9	13.6
★ 3	20	30.3	9	13.6	37	56.1
4	55	84.6	4	6.2	6	9.2
★ 5	15	22.7	11	16.7	40	60.6
6	40	61.5	22	33.9	3	4.6
★ 7	10	15.6	7	10.9	47	73.5
★ 8	11	16.9	15	23.1	39	60.0
9	61	93.8	4	6.2	0	0.0
10	52	78.8	13	19.7	1	1.5
11	46	71.9	13	20.3	5	7.8
★ 12	16	24.6	22	33.9	27	41.5
13	41	68.3	9	15.0	10	16.7
14	54	83.1	6	9.2	5	7.7
15	39	60.0	17	26.2	9	13.8
16	53	80.3	10	15.2	3	4.5
17	52	81.3	10	15.6	2	3.1
18	50	76.9	9	13.9	6	9.2
19	45	70.3	15	23.4	4	6.3
20	42	64.6	16	24.6	7	10.8

★ Note: Starred items were phrased negatively.

★★ Item numbers correspond to statements on PFEI (Figure 13.2).

It can be seen that the students tended to view the experience as a positive one. The results suggest that both the process and the outcomes were favorable. Closer examination of items 1-10, however, enabled the peer facilitators to gain some insight into what took place. It is important to note that not all the students were positive in their assessment of the process. Some thought that others did not listen to them and some felt that not everyone participated in the group. A few concluded that the peer facilitators with whom they worked were not interested in them. Some were "neutral" or perhaps unsure of what happened.

Nevertheless, the study clearly suggests that the experience was, in general, positive for the majority of students and that, more often than not, the students perceived the peer facilitators and the group as doing those things that are considered "facilitative." In this case it is easy to see how the process was related to the positive outcomes (11-20).

In this study of elementary school students, approximately 72% indicated that the experience had helped change their attitudes and 83% found school to be more enjoyable. A large majority (81.1%) got to know other students better, while approximately 77% felt they understood each other better.

An understanding of self also increased (70.1%). Forty-two of the sixty-six students (64.1%) reported that they perceived some change in their behavior as a result of their experiences in the group. It is certainly a success story for those peer facilitators who gave of their time and energy to work with the young students. The collected data, although limited in some respects, provides concrete evidence that the program and the peer intervention was effective.

A similar study was also conducted with twenty-eight ninth and tenth graders at the same high school which the peers attended. These students were taken randomly and voluntarily from English, general science and social adjustment classes. They participated in some small group discussions led by co-facilitators. Their perceptions of the process and the outcomes can be seen in *Table III*. Again, it will be noted that the process and resulting outcomes were positive.

In this case, the majority of students reported that they got to know themselves and others better. More than 1 out of 2 students (53.1%) thought the group helped them change their attitudes about some things. Two out of five (40.1%) indicated that the group helped change their behavior. All but three recommended the experience for others.

Table III

RESPONSES BY SECONDARY SCHOOL
STUDENTS TO THE PFEI

(N=28)

Item Number★ ★	Positive (SA+A)		Undecided (U)		Negative (D+SD)	
	Frequency	%	Frequency	%	Frequency	%
1	23	82.1	0	0.0	5	17.9
2	20	71.4	7	25.0	1	3.6
★ 3	16	57.1	3	10.7	9	32.2
4	18	64.2	5	17.9	5	17.9
★ 5	10	35.7	1	3.6	17	60.7
6	15	53.6	6	21.4	7	25.0
★ 7	5	17.9	0	0.0	23	82.1
★ 8	3	10.7	7	25.0	18	64.3
9	24	85.7	1	3.6	3	10.7
10	21	75.0	1	3.6	6	21.4
11	15	53.6	5	17.8	8	28.6
★ 12	10	35.7	10	35.7	8	28.6
13	5	18.5	4	14.8	18	66.7
14	12	42.9	5	17.9	11	39.3
15	16	57.2	6	21.4	6	21.4
16	23	82.1	2	7.2	3	10.7
17	20	71.4	3	10.7	5	17.9
18	21	75.0	3	10.7	4	14.3
19	17	60.7	4	14.3	7	25.0
20	11	40.8	7	25.9	9	33.3

★ NOTE: Starred items were phrased negatively.

★ ★ Item numbers correspond to statements on PFEI (Figure 13.2).

Discussing the Findings

When discussing the results of an inventory such as the PFEI, you will find that your students frequently want to know more about those who reported the experience to be less exciting and helpful than others. The tendency is to analyze the failures, to fret over criticism.

First, it should be remembered that there is always a chance for an error in measurement or for someone to misunderstand the directions and mark the instrument incorrectly. On the other hand, there will be occasions when one or two simply find the experience questionable.

For example, of the sixty-six students in one of the studies previously cited, only one student reported that the peer facilitators seemed unenthusiastic. Is this an error? An exception? Even if it is not, it would be unfortunate if the peer facilitator class spent the majority of their time trying to understand that one response. Fifty-two students clearly saw them as enthusiastic. Focus on the positive as much as possible!

While we are concerned about those who are less responsive to a peer intervention project than others, it is important to take gaines where we get them and to recognize them as significant.

GROUP EVALUATION FORM (GEF).

Another form that has been used to help assess both process and outcomes of different group experiences is the *Group Evaluation Form* (Figure 13.3). This simple form also uses the Likert-type response set (Strongly Agree to Strongly Disagree) and provides a measure of peer facilitator effectiveness. This particular instrument is less detailed than the PFEI, but still can be useful.

Figure 13.3

GROUP EVALUATION FORM

I. Read each of the statements below. Indicate the extent of your agreement or disagreement with each statement by circling the appropriate letters to the right: SA—Strongly Agree; A—Agree; U—Uncertain; D—Disagree; SD—Strongly Disagree. Please respond to all of the statements.

1. The group helped change my behavior outside the group.   SA A U D SD

2. I would recommend a similar group experience for others.   SA A U D SD

3. The group helped me clarify some of my beliefs, attitudes and values.   SA A U D SD

4. I enjoyed being a member of the group.   SA A U D SD

5. As a result of the group, I feel more comfortable with some of my classmates.   SA A U D SD

Research Based on the GEF

Forty-nine eighth grade students met in groups of seven for fifteen sessions with high school peer facilitators. Each group was co-led by two facilitators. Following completion of the sessions, the middle school students were asked to complete anonymously the *Group Evaluation Form*. The results are reported in *Table IV*. It can be seen that the experience was a positive one for the vast majority of the students and that 98% would recommend the group to others. In addition to the five statements where students indicated their agreement or disagreement, the open-ended questions also provide interesting data. Some sample responses to "I learn that I. . ." can be seen in *Table IV*.

Table IV

RESPONSES BY MIDDLE SCHOOL STUDENTS TO THE GEF

(N=49)

Item Number ★	Positive (SA+A)		Undecided (U)		Negative (D+SD)	
	Frequency	%	Frequency	%	Frequency	%
1	26	53	17	35	12	6
2	48	98	1	2	-	0
3	32	65	17	35	-	0
4	30	60	17	35	5	2
5	34	70	11	22	8	4

★ Item numbers correspond to statements on *Group Evaluation Form* (Figure 13.3).

The following are samples of their responses to the unfinished sentence, I learned that I. . .

> . . . could feel comfortable with other people.
> . . . had friends.
> . . . am very understanding and friendly.
> . . . am needed by others.
> . . . need to stick with my ideas and beliefs more.
> . . . can work with others.
> . . . cared for my parents.
> . . . am someone to other people.
> . . . value many things.
> . . . should open up more to others.
> . . . can get along with almost anybody.
> . . . could be a little better around others.
> . . . can make friends easily.
> . . . can trust people.
> . . . could speak comfortably to a group.
> . . . was interested in people.
> . . . like to be alone.
> . . . am important!
> . . . know myself pretty well.
> . . . can do more things.
> . . . like to listen to people.
> . . . am special.

In another study, fifty high school students were randomly selected from a sociology and psychology class. These students, grades 10-12, participated in a guidance unit that involved one of the school counselors and ten peer facilitators as discussion leaders.

They first met with the students in one large group where the counselor presented some general information regarding career and educational planning. Life skills and the need for self-awareness were also discussed.

After the initial presentation in each session, the large group was divided into groups of ten students each. Two facilitators, serving as co-leaders, joined each group. After working together for eight sessions (twice a week for four weeks), the *Group Evaluation Form* (Figure 13.3) was administered. The results are found in *Table V.*

Table V
RESPONSES BY HIGH SCHOOL STUDENTS TO THE GEF

(N=50)

Item Number★	Positive (SA+A)		Undecided (U)		Negative (D+SD)	
	Frequency	%	Frequency	%	Frequency	%
1	14	28	22	44	14	28
2	40	80	8	15	2	4
3	35	70	8	15	7	14
4	40	80	8	15	2	4
5	29	58	I9	38	2	4

★ Item numbers correspond to statements on *Group Evaluation Form* (Figure 13.3).

The following are samples of their responses to the unfinished sentence:

I learned that I . . .

. . . was unable to share my thoughts.
. . . really did't know myself until this group.
. . . can find more out about people if I listen to them.
. . . didn't know myself like I want.
. . . was able to talk openly.
. . . really like being with other people.
. . . am changing.
. . . am a person who enjoys life.
. . . am not so different form others.
. . . can learn to get along better with others by finding out what they feel.

Approximately 65% believed that the experience helped them clarify their beliefs, attitudes and values. Another 70% agreed that the group helped them feel more comfortable with some of their classmates and 98% recommended the group for others.

Obviously, this form can be designed to meet a particular trainer or peer facilitator's interests. The statements can be changed to meet your specific needs. Some other statements regarding process and some regarding more specific outcomes could be included. Regardless, such a measure can provide for a systematic collection of information and the results could be tabulated to give some picture of an experience, no matter what the intervention might be.

SYSTEMATIC CASE STUDY

The *Ststematic Case Study* (*Caring and Sharing*, Chapter VII) is a unique method for collecting data. It can describe both process and outcomes. When a collaborative approach is used in which several peer facilitators use the same kind of criterion measures, the findings can be pooled and the results are usually impressive.

DIRECT OBSERVATION

When behavior can be directly observed, recorded and studied, the report of outcomes can be even more impressive. However, many programs find that it is not practical or feasible to arrange an elaborate research design or use sophisticated procedures to help them establish credibility. While recognizing limitations, these programs can still benefit from some kind of accounting procedure.

INDEPENDENT OBSERVERS

Sometimes it is helpful to ask others who are not directly involved in the process to report their observations. For example, teachers and hosts of peer facilitators are excellent sources of information because they have many opportunities to observe the facilitators and the students with whom they are working. They can offer some "objective" points of view that are useful.

There are many measures that can be used by "independent observers" to help collect information. Some are more complex than others. Perhaps the very best instruments concentrate on specific behaviors that can be observed and recorded. They avoid generalizations or labels. For example, instead of saying: "is cooperative" or "classroom behavior has improved," it might be better to provide an item that is more specific and related to those general conclusions: "completes work on time," "participates in class discussions" or "follows directions and classroom guidelines." This more specific focus requires the observer to concentrate on one particular behavior.

One example of a measure which attempts to let others report their impressions of peer facilitators' work and their experience with the program is found in Figure 13.4. It follows the now familiar format of the Likert-type scale and enables the respondent to communicate agreement or disagreement with each statement. Space is also provided for answers to open-ended questions.

Figure 13.4

TEACHER/HOST PEER FACILITATOR EVALUATION FORM

To: Peer Facilitator Hosts

From: Tom Erney

I am interested in learning more about your feelings and ideas regarding the peer facilitator(s) who worked with students in your class. I am interested in knowing their level of performance and what might be done to improve our efforts. Please complete this form and return it to the counselor in your school. I will collect them and be happy to talk with anyone who wants to discuss the program or the peer facilitators' work in greater detail. Thanks for your help and interest.

Tom

CIRCLE ONE:

SA—Strongly Agree; A—Agree; U—Uncertain; D—Disagree;
SD—Strongly Disagree

1. I am glad that I chose to have a facilita-   SA A U D SD
tor work in my class.

2. I feel as though the facilitators have   SA A U D SD
been well-trained.

3. The students look forward to the   SA A U D SD
facilitators being in class.

4. I *doubt* if the faciltators really ac-   SA A U D SD
complish anything worthwhile.

PLEASE COMPLETE THE FOLLOWING STATEMENTS:

5. If *other teachers* would ask me about the peer facilitators, I
would say the following:

6. One *suggestion* I would like to make is. . . .

7. One *concern* I have is. . . .

SUMMARY

There are numerous criterion instruments that might be
employed in an accountability study. Some of these are standardized and some are not. Because the concept is relatively
new, there are not many standardized measures which focus
specifically on the work of peer facilitators. This should not
deter you from systematically collecting data.

Though limited, trainer-developed instruments like those reported here are valuable. These kinds of instruments frequently
prove to be clear and meaningful to the majority of people who
are in the school and community. Administrators, professional
colleagues and the general public can appreciate the difficulty
of conducting a thorough and sophisticated research project.
These same people also appreciate the opportunity to "see"
and study the data that is available.

In particular, the kind of information described in this chapter
has proven helpful in making presentations to school boards
and the general public. Accountability measures are the step-
ping-stones for positive public relations.

PROMOTING YOUR PROGRAM

Maintaining and expanding a support system often depends upon being able to effectively communicate your program to others. Here are some more ways to promote public relations:

(1) Parent Meetings

> You may want to hold some of these during the year in order to keep the parents informed and to request any assistance that you may need.

(2) Luncheons/Dinners

> Approximately once a month, the peer facilitators at Buchholz High School in Gainesville, Florida have a noon-time meal at one of the facilitator's homes. Students "pitch-in" by signing up to bring salads, drinks, meat and so on. The host family has a minimum of responsibilities. The faciltators usually go to the house during classtime, which is scheduled for the period before lunch.

> Such an activity can promote group cohesiveness and provide an opportunity for the host parent(s) to experience how cooperative and "special" the peer facilitators are. The parents will be impressed with the group.

(3) Speeches

> Most community groups are looking for an interesting program to present for their members. Groups such as the Kiwanis, Lions, Rotary, Parent-Teacher Organizations and the Chamber of Commerce, to mention just a few, might welcome a call volunteering the services of you and your students to speak at one of their meetings.

> Let your peer facilitators handle much of the presentation. They will prove to be impressive spokespersons and will sell your program through their enthusiasm and involvement.

(4) Professional Presentations

The peer facilitator concept has been popular at local, state and national conventions. Share your enthusiasm and ideas with your peers.

(5) Newspaper Articles

The local newspaper is perhaps the most effective means of letting large numbers of people in your community know of your program and its benefits. Stories illustrating the positive work of young people are well-received and can generate a great amount of local support.

"Telling and selling others" is a vital part of your role as a trainer of peer facilitators. It should not be neglected or overlooked. When you systematically collect supporting data of facilitators' effectiveness, you can improve aspects of your program and convincingly describe its positive impact.

Chapter XIV

the new helpers: a revolution in school guidance

No matter how much school teachers, counselors and psychologists have tried, there are still many children and young adults who have unfulfilled counseling and guidance needs. These needs are so extensive and varied that they cannot be met without a comprehensive and effective school guidance program. Moreover, as it becomes more apparent that these needs will not be met by a single set of services or one type of helping person, guidance programs will experience significant changes. One of these changes is the diversification of roles, functions and levels of responsibility.

THE PARAPROFESSIONAL MOVEMENT

During the last decade, the use of support personnel received special attention. The term "paraprofessional" emerged and has been used to describe a "non-credentialed person" who performs tasks that are directly related to guidance. Most important, without the presence of this paraprofessional, the task would probably be performed by a member of the professional counseling staff. After a somewhat shaky and critical start, it appears that the paraprofessional is now seen as an important part of most guidance programs.

TO BE OR NOT TO BE?

Paraprofessionals are able to offer numerous services to a school program. However, the extent of their involvement generally depends on the views of the professional staff. A review of the professional literature suggests that paraprofessionals have not always been welcomed as members of the guidance team. To the contrary, there was much criticism when they were used as counseling aides. Part of the criticism was because there was some confusion as to exactly what their role would be.

Blaker, Schmidt and Jensen (1971) conducted a survey in order to discover the extent to which paraprofessionals or counselor aides were being used in various guidance programs. Responses were obtained from 129 high schools and 60 community colleges. They learned that paraprofessionals were used mainly to provide clerical assistance and were often responsible for maintaining career and college information libraries. In general, community colleges have used paraprofessionals in "outreach programs" and they have had more student contact than have most high schools.

Steenland (1973) surveyed university and college counseling centers to find out what use they were making of undergraduates who were working as paraprofesional counselors. Services included: 1) a crisis center or telephone "hot line"; 2) study skills help; 3) a companionship program, such as Big Brothers/Sisters; 4) test administration; 5) some peer counseling in the area of student adjustment and orientation.

The use of paraprofessionals also enabled some colleges and universities to develop new programs to meet student needs. For example, Allen (1974) described six programs on a single college campus that were staffed entirely with paraprofessionals. The student paraprofessionals received training in interpersonal skills and also some specific training for the particular job or program in which they were working.

TRAINING AND SUPERVISION

Despite these successes, criticism has continued. Some professional counselors believe that the work of paraprofessionals should be limited and that, without training, they should not be allowed to work with students in a "counseling" situation. Some counselors also perceive the paraprofessional as an economic threat, believing that they are less expensive and could, if successful, take the place of certified personnel.

In addition, there is some question as to who is responsible for supervising the paraprofessional and for the outcomes of the paraprofessional's work. It was feared that without appropriate training, paraprofessionals might do more harm than be of service.

While investigating the concept of essential therapeutic qualities related to counseling effectiveness, Carkhuff (1966, 1968) built a case for the use of the paraprofessional. He found them to be as effective as professional personnel, especially if they have been trained to function at high facilitative levels.

Despite the criticism of some skeptics, Poser (1966) suggested that the effective ingredients in an interpersonal relationship were uniquely human and independent of training. It follows that if a person seemed to emit the characteristics of a helping relationship, no counseling training was needed before the person could "counsel" with others. In addition, Shapiro and Voog (1969) provided further evidence that certain individuals seem to have the necessary therapeutic qualities which enable them, without training, to facilitate others.

EFFECTIVENESS

Before paraprofessionals could really be accepted as part of a guidance program, some evidence of their effectiveness was needed. During the past several years, there have been several studies which suggest that paraprofessionals can be and have been effective.

For instance, Truax and Lister (1970) compared the effectiveness of rehabilitation counselors and untrained counselor-aides under three conditions: counselor alone, counselor with an aide and aide alone. Findings indicated that the greatest client improvement occured when aides worked alone with the clients. The least amount of client improvement resulted when professional counselors and aides worked together. These results are consistent with those obtained with lay mental health counselors (Carkhuff and Truax, 1965) and untrained group psycho-therapists (Poser, 1966).

Still other studies of paraprofessionals' effectiveness have been positive. Riessman and Gartner (1969) studied 1000 programs for disadvantaged students between 1963 and 1968. Of these, 23 were found to have measurable benefits and, of these, 11 involved the use of paraprofessionals.

Vander Kolk (1973) described an interesting program where teacher aides were trained to act as therapeutic agents with moderately disturbed children. The training program involved three one-hour sessions. During the first session, the training focused on building helping relationships and the helpers' responsibilities to children as therapeutic agents. In the second session, attention was given to: possible problems; how to begin and develop a helping relationship; and the importance of confidentiality. Case studies were the subject of discussion in the third session.

As part of this same study, 40 students were randomly drawn from a list of 56 teacher referrals. Twenty of the students were randomly assigned to an experimental group and the other twenty were designated as controls. The experimental group did not show a noticeable change in self-esteem, as measured by a standardized inventory. But, in the meantime, the control group was falling behind.

One of the most interesting parts of the study, however, was when the subjects were grouped according to "most" versus "least" amount of time spent with paraprofessionals. Interestingly enough, those who spent the "most time" with the trained paraprofessionals made the most significant gain in self-esteem. In addition, there was some perceived improvement in the children who experienced help by the teacher aides.

As the evidence of paraprofessional effectiveness has increased, there has been a paralleling increase in the number of training programs. Moreover, these training programs are now better organized and more systematic. Perhaps the greatest number of programs today still focus on helping paraprofessionals prepare for work at colleges and universities and in community agencies. Part of this expansion can be explained because of the increased amount of federal funding available to employ paraprofessional personnel.

SOME IMPORTANT ISSUES

The development and growth of the paraprofessional movement laid the foundation for peer counselors and peer facilitators. Because they are viewed as "support personnel" in a guidance program, there are some important issues that are parallel to the paraprofessional movement.

Among these are: What functions are to be performed? How much training is needed? Who supervises the paraprofessional or peer facilitator? What personal qualities should these facilitators have?

Trainers of peer facilitators will most likely find that these questions will persist for some time. Until paraprofessional positions and peer facilitator programs are firmly established, there will continue to be a number of unanswered questions.

Paraprofessionals are used in many different ways across the nation. This is also true of students who work as peer counselors or peer facilitators. Responsibilities vary. The amount of assistance also varies. Most important, training of these "new helpers" is also diverse. The idea of youth helping youth is intriguing and the potential impact is most appealing.

THE PEER FACILITATOR MOVEMENT

STUDENTS AS TUTORS

Students have long been used as "tutors" to help other students. For instance, high school students have helped their peers improve scholastic performance in reading (McCleary, 1971; Shaver and Nuhn, 1971); mathematics (Caditz, 1963); English (Lobitz, 1970) and business education (Van Wagenen, 1969). In a study by Weitzman (1965), students who received tutoring help from other students performed better on reports, essays, homework and general assignments. Tutored students did not differ significantly from non-tutored students in examinations or quizes.

One of the best known and most widely discussed tutoring projects has come from the Detroit, Michigan area (Lippitt and Lohman, 1965; Lippitt and Lippitt, 1968; Lippitt and Lippitt, 1970). Fourth grade children with reading difficulties were tutored by sixth grade children. It was learned that the older students benefited from the experience. It was recommended that student-to-student contact should be from 20-60 minutes a day and for three or four days a week. In addition, it was suggested that older students needed some kind of in-service training and that the "tutor" should confer with the younger students' ('tutees') teacher on a regular basis.

In many cases, tutors provide more than simple drill or explanation. More often than not, the primary focus is to provide a helping relationship in the form of a "big brother/ sister." Norris and Wantland (1972) reported how "big brothers and sisters" volunteered to help younger classmates in reading. In addition, Baker (1963) explained that a "big friend" program used children ages 9 to 13 to work with younger children ages 5 to 8 in both reading and mathematics. *Both of these reports claimed benefits to tutors as well as to tutees.*

It is not uncommon to find that tutors gain signficantly from helping tutees. Cloward (1967) found significant gains in the reading scores of tutors over a five month period in which older children tutored younger children with reading difficulties. The tutees gained six months in reading level while the tutors gained 3.4 years!

Likewise, Erickson and Cromack (1972) used underachieving seventh grade students to tutor underachieving third grade students. When change patterns in reading performance were examined and compared to those of classmates, the results suggested that the tutees and the tutors improved significantly.

Frager and Stein (1970) also used high and low achieving sixth grade students to tutor kindergarten children. Once again, results indicated that the tutors were effective in helping kindergarten children in language readiness, as compared to a control group. Besides making language gains, absenteeism was reduced among the children who were tutored. But again, it is important to note that the tutors also gained. Their attitude towards school improved as well as their attendance. Still other studies (Lane, Pollack & Sher, 1972 ; Geiser, l969; Fredicine & Kramer, 1971; Lundburg, 1968; Porter, 1971; Rossi, 1969; Vassallo, 1973) have reported positive effects among tutors as well as tutees.

With these studies in mind, it is appropriate to focus on an important concept of peer facilitator programs. Even though the intention of a program is to provide services to someone outside that program—such as a younger student—the evidence continues to suggest that *training is treatment*. Thus, *a peer facilitator program can be an alternative intervention in a guidance and counseling program.*

Some trainers of peer facilitators have reported situations in which students are deliberately recruited to be part of the program because it was hypothesized that they would gain as much as anyone that they were assigned to help. In these cases, the students are usually potential leaders. Their abilities have usually not been recognized or encouraged. Regardless, we can not ignore the idea that students help students in many ways and that the helping process is not a one-way street.

STUDENTS AS AIDES

Besides tutoring other students in academic subjects, students have been used as aides to teachers and counselors at all levels. While this role is not a new one, it is generally more expanded than it has been in the past. Students are having more direct contact with other students.

As aides or classroom assistants, students have proven to be a valuable resource. Christine (1971) reported that of 128 school systems studied who were using students as assistants, only four reported negative results and most indicated a desire for increased services in the future. It was further reported that lack of funds appeared to prevent the use of more paraprofessionals and student aides.

As counselor aides, students have assisted in orienting new students to school. In conducting tours, as well as giving some general information, peers have proven to be helpful. Aides have assisted in developing materials, organizing bulletin boards and writing articles for the school newspaper. They have helped with research activities, such as administration of tests and surveys. They have been responsible for initial interviews, presentations in auditoriums and classrooms— helping other students learn more about the guidance program. In some cases they have served as models and reinforcing agents in order to improve peer social acceptance and interaction (Lilly, 1971).

While it has been recognized for many years that students can be a valuable source of support as aides or assistants, it has only been in recent years that more systematic efforts have been made to put students in a "counseling or facilitator" role. This new use of students as helpers has been a revolution in education.

STUDENTS AS PEER COUNSELORS AND FACILITATORS

The research and literature related to paraprofessional workers has helped stimulate new developments in guidance, including peer counseling and peer facilitator programs. Among the reasons why such programs have come into existence are:

(1) The number of certified professional counselors is limited and the needs of students are more extensive than most professional staffs can meet.

(2) Students provide a practical and economical means for meeting the increasing number of guidance and counseling needs.

(3) Research indicates that student counselors and facilitators can often be as effective as professional counselors in many guidance activities.

(4) Evidence also indicates that student facilitators are as accepted by student "clients" as are professional counselors. In some cases they are accepted even more so, especially in the initial stages of developing a relationship.

(5) With some groups, particularly minorities, developing trust and credibility between students and those associated with the educational establishment—teachers, administrators and counselors— has been a problem. Students tend to trust other students more. Minority counselors or therapists are relatively few in number and minority students often avoid traditional mental health services.

(6) Sometimes information can be presented to students in an informal and less intimidating manner when peers provide the information.

(7) Many times adults do not understand the straight-forward language and customs of the younger generation. Student facilitators can help bridge this gap and assist older professionals in gaining a better perspective on student problems and issues.

(8) The range of guidance services can be extended in a school when peers are used as resources.

(9) A peer facilitator program provides an "outreach" approach to guidance, which is most appropriate for contemporary times.

(10) Peer facilitators can function as models within a work or educational setting.

(11) Learning is more efficient when students assist other students and accept more responsibility for creating the learning climate.

(12) "Training is treatment." The facilitator gains from being a facilitator of others.

(13) Peer facilitator programs are the heart of a developmental approach to guidance and counseling. In developmental guidance programs, life skills are developed prior to a crisis. Many times crises are avoided because stress and tension are reduced.

PEER TRAINING: COLLEGE LEVEL

For these and other reasons, more attention is being given to the training of peer facilitators. Several studies record the use of students as peer facilitators and counselors at the college level. Many of the studies have focused on academic and social learning.

Ettkin and Snyder (1972) reported a model for peer-group counseling based on role playing. The method consisted of four three-hour group sessions which involved role playing situations that were perceived as threatening to the group members. The group identified a stressful situation of interest to the group and then selected a presenter, a protagonist and an alter-ego. The stage was set for the presentation and the play took place. Later, roles were reversed. After each role played situation, the leader encouraged the discussion of ideas and feelings aroused by the play.

Simpson, Pate and Burks (1973) used students as beginning vocational counselors in both individual and group studies. The training was systematic in that the student first learned some basic ideas through video-tapes of counselors who served as models. Particular attention was given to helping the "peer counselors" reach a level of expertise so that some counseling tasks could be performed.

Brown (1965) described a 40-hour training program which consisted of organized activities involving skills in orientation, academic instruction and educational planning. After training, student counselors met for three two-hour sessions with college freshmen. Findings indicated that freshmen counseled by students scored significantly higher than a control group on a measure of study behavior. The counseled students also earned higher grades during their first semester of school.

An important study by Zunker and Brown (1966) compared the effectiveness of student and professional counselors. Professional and student counselors completed 50 hours of identical precounseling training which was made up of lectures, demonstrations, discussions and practice sessions. Identical guidance materials and counseling activities were also used (i.e. orientation program, test interpretation, student habits and study skills).

Examination of research findings indicated that student counselors were as effective as professional counselors, based on scholarship data an a questionnaire. Moreover, those counseled by students made greater use of the information received, retained the information longer and evaluated the counseling program higher. Another important finding was that those students who were counseled by "student counselors" accepted counseling more readily.

PEER TRAINING: SECONDARY SCHOOLS

Perhaps because students are older and more mature, the use of "peer counselors" in colleges and universities preceded the use of "peer counselors" at the secondary and elementary school levels. There were, of course, some early attempts to develop peer leadership programs in the schools and there were some interesting developments regarding guidance activities, but these efforts were limited.

Vriend (1969) developed a program for peer counseling in an inter-city school. Drawing upon high-performing achievers as peer leaders, group discussions were organized and the peer leaders were used to support behaviors associated with achievement. Later, large groups were divided into smaller study groups, each with one peer leader. These groups met for three forty-minute periods per week to implement the activities planned in the large group sessions.

Information was given about careers. There were some efforts made to focus on self-evaluation and self-improvement. Using grade point averages as one criterion, there was a significant difference between a group of students who worked with peers, as opposed to those that did not. In addition, students who worked with peer leaders also improved in their attendance and punctuality.

One of the first places to use peers as counselors, and to receive national recognition, was in the secondary schools of Palo Alto, California (Hamburg & Varenhorst, 1971, 1972; & Varenhorst, 1973). After advertising for students, those who were interested in becoming peer counselors were admitted to a training program. As student leaders, they were to assist other students in solving personal problems, teach social skills and act as models. They also were to develop friendships and help bridge the communication gap between students and adults.

The training program consisted of small group discussions with a professional supervisor. These supervisors (four school psychologists, five psychiatrists, a guidance director and an English teacher) met regularly to develop a training curriculum and to evaluate the progress of the program. The training program focused on three basic areas: 1) understanding people, 2) topics relevant to peer counseling and 3) strategies used in counseling. There was also a practicum experience.

The first four training meetings dealt with understanding people. Session one focused on the purpose and structure for the group. Student leaders were to keep participants on a topic of discussion. One person was designated "observer" and withdrew from the group. During the last 20 minutes, the group listened and reacted to feedback from the observer. The supervisor, in the meantime, modeled appropriate leader behaviors, presented materials and summarized. The second through the fourth sessions dealt with communication skills and special attention was given to one-to-one relationships and group dynamics.

The next four training meetings involved counseling topics. During the fifth session, academic motivation received attention. The sixth meeting covered adolescent problems such as drug use, emotional disturbance, physical handicaps, unwanted pregnancy, ethical differences and racial differences. In the seventh meeting, family problems received attention: divorce, restrictions, expectations, sibling rivalry, death, moving into a new environment and punishment. A discussion of plans, goals and career alternatives occured in the eighth meeting. To aid the discussions in these sessions, personal attitudes and experiences of friends were shared. Other sources which proved helpful in stimulating discussions were cases studies, role playing and specific information on such topics as family therapy, drug abuse, abortion counseling and vocational opportunities.

One of the unique aspects of this early program was the "practicum experience." Peer counselors were assigned to work with sixth grade students in small groups, without adult supervision. Each group discussed feelings about transition from elementary to junior high school. Throughout the training sessions, students practiced "counseling" with one another. They reviewed ethical responsibilities and differentiated between counseling and advice-giving.

Counseling was viewed as being a process of exploration of alternatives, with final decisions for action being the counselee's responsibility. Although research and evaluation of this particular program has been somewhat limited, recognition has been deserved because of the manner in which the training program was organized. This program, along with a few others, helped establish the principle that peers need training and supervision. It emphasized that hundreds of students can be served through such a program.

Leibowitz and Rhodes (1974) described an adolescent peer program that was organized around group procedures and role playing. A supervised practicum was the primary focus for learning. Twelve peer counselors were selected from applicants on the basis of faculty recommendations and personal interviews. The training sessions took place one a week for $2^1/2$ hours and continued for nine weeks.

The first four sessions were designed to improve listening and counseling skills. The next three sessions focused on responding skills as related to decision-making and the formulation of counseling goals. The final two training sessions centered on supervision. Recorded peer counseling tapes were critiqued in small groups. Using pre and post tests levels of empathic understanding, the contention that high school students could learn to develop high levels of empathic understanding and could provide a helping relationship to peers was supported.

Another type of training program for peer counselors was reported by Sprinthall and Erickson (1974). In this case, high school students were offered a course in which they learned listening skills and empathic responses. Role playing exercises were used and a practicum was organized.

Samuels and Samuels (1975) described a peer counseling program which was particularly designed to help curb drug abuse. This program was started in Miami, Florida and students followed an organized set of activities. The program for training "peer counselors," however, could apply to peer facilitators who work in other settings.

More recently, Gray and Tindall (1978) published a student work book and a trainer manual. These materials grew out of their interest in training paraprofessionals. Drawing upon the ideas and concepts developed by Dreikurs, Carkhuff and Sprinthall, a systematic training program is outlined. Students are provided exercises which help them learn more about human relations.

Attention is also given to the role of a trainer and the development of a "peer counseling" program. One skill is built sequentially upon another. They begin with the issue of attending, communication stoppers and building empathy. Summarizing, questioning, confronting and being genuine are then discussed. Finally, problem-solving is outlined. Gray and Tindall also describe the use of peer counselors in different settings.

No doubt there are many other outstanding peer facilitator or counseling programs throughout the United States. Some of these have received more attention than others because they have been part of a presentation at national conventions. Others have been described in professional publications or given some state grant which led to a final report. Unfortunately, there are many outstanding programs that have not been described in professional literature and, thus, knowledge of them is limited.

One such outstanding effort is the peer counseling program in the Baltimore City Public Schools. It started as part of a ESEA Title II grant in 1974 and was entitled "Student Facilitators in the Guidance Process." The term "student facilitator" is used. Initially, it involved six pilot schools, including two senior high schools, two junior high schools and two elementary schools.

The ESEA funds provided a work-study program whereby students were paid a minimum wage and received academic credit in a class called "Social Psychology." The program was open to interested students, fourteen years or older. Students were selected on the basis of observed "high status in peer relationships," expressed interest, satisfactory academic achievement commensurate with ability and teacher recommendations. A cross-section of students was also a basic goal in selection.

Once students are chosen, they are required to complete thirty hours of intensive study in both verbal and non-verbal communication skills. This includes listening, values clarification, referral techniques, decison-making skills and confidentiality. Role playing is a primary method for teaching skills.

Training sessions are conducted on Saturdays and after school on Wednesdays. Upon completion of the training, students are then placed in a middle or elementary school. Each day for one scheduled class period, student facilitators work with their peers and younger students. Weekly supervision sessions are scheduled and attendance is required. The weekly session provides support and encouragement. Skills are examined and additional information provided when needed.

These peer facilitators work with school adjustment and attendance problems. They help disseminate college information and help students learn to use their time more wisely. They try to build self-confidence and motivate students by offering rapsessions and serving as role models.

In 1978, Baltimore was awarded an ESEA Title IV, Part C grant in order to promote the program state-wide. The project is entitled *PROMISE—Peer Reach Out for Maryland Involving Students and Educators*. Guidance and counseling supervisors, coordinators and directors are participating in state-wide workshops in order to help the program reach more students (Bell, 1978).

Another interesting program that is training young people to help each other is a project entitled *Responsibility Education Through Peer Facilitation*. This project (Title IV, ESEA) is part of the Meridian School District in Mounds, Illinois.

The project was designed to stimulate student responsibility and to assist students in becoming more knowledgeable about decision-making strategies based upon alternatives and consequences. In particular, this program provides highly structured training sessions for peer facilitators and a model for working in rural and high minority areas.

Approximatley 15-20 students in grades nine through twelve take part in a class that provides a half-unit of academic credit in the area of social studies. In the near future, this project will also be evaluated and disseminated to other schools in the state of Illinois.

The P. K. Yonge Laboratory School, University of Florida, has developed a program entitled *Adopt an Athlete*. It has made "brothers and sisters of nearly 1,000 elementary students and 150 athletes since 1973.

According to Don McFadyen, the coach: "We were looking for ways to enhance school spirit and to make our football games and other athletic events real for children. The adoption program was a natural off-shoot. We decided to have the children in an elementary class adopt one football player as their big brother. In one year alone 250 children in grades K-5 adopted 40 junior and senior high school varsity football players and cheerleaders. The adoption program is now being expanded to include other sports and team members."

The players visit the elementary classes throughout the year and help out with academics. Sometimes they work with children who are trying to express hurt feelings. Many develop close relationships.

In the Littleton School District of Denver, Colorado, students are selected to be in a "Positive Peer Program." They wear large buttons with the initials "PPP" which indentifies them to other students in the student body. These students were trained to be student facilitators through a service of "retreat workshops."

Two- and three-day "retreats" were held and outside consultants instructed them in the use of interpersonal skills. The program director followed these workshops with a special training session during the school hours. The peer facilitators are assigned "duty hours" in the guidance office and are viewed as an adjunct to the counseling program.

"Retreat workshops" are very effective and are particularly desirable when school time is limited for training. Training can be compressed into a weekend workshop, but follow up or "refresher" sessions are necessary.

SUMMARY

While peer facilitators and peer counselors are relatively new on the school guidance scene, there are growing numbers of programs in existence across the nation. Outstanding programs can be identified by the following conditions: 1) a selection process that provides a representative picture of the student body; 2) a systematic training process; 3) field experiences that "reach out"; 4) supervision; 5) a focus on the facilitation of learning conditions in the classrooms around the school; and 6) involvement of teachers, parents and administrators.

Chapter XV

the trainer as facilitator and learner

Being the person responsible for the training and supervision of peer facilitators is a challenging and rewarding, personal learning experience. It is challenging because of the interpersonal skills that must be taught, the questions that demand answers and the decisions that must be made. It is rewarding because it enhances the lives of hundreds of young people who experience some very special attention and caring as a result of the program. Finally, it is a personal learning experience for the trainers because the trainers must re-evaluate their professional skills, develop new ones and, at the same time, clarify their own values systems.

What are the characteristics of a successful peer facilitator trainer?

A SUCCESSFUL PEER FACILITATOR TRAINER IS . . .

. . . KNOWLEDGEABLE ABOUT HUMAN BEHAVIOR.

Being a trainer requires a basic knowledge of human behavior and interpersonal relationships. Being knowledgeable does not mean being an "expert" or "all-knowing." In addition, you will want to avoid becoming dependent upon one set of theoretical concepts. When training young people, it is especially important to be practical and straight-forward. Identify the fundamental ideas and concepts and relate them to "real-life" situations. Give clear examples. Theories that can be put into practice will be most useful.

The basic ideas and concepts presented in this book have stood the test for applicability and simplicity. They serve as the foundation upon which a program can be built. They offer stability and continuity. But, they are not meant as a final answer or solution. Your knowledge of human behavior, interpersonal relationships and helping techniques can add strength to this foundation.

. . . ORGANIZED AND PLANS AHEAD.

Students helping other students is not a new idea. What *is* new, however, is the systematic training of students as "facilitators" and their use in more challenging roles. A carefully planned and supervised program can provide direction and prevent the frustration that often accompanies sincere, but unorganized, attempts to help others. The security that results from planning and organizing can enable you and others to be more confident.

Develop a plan of action. You have, of course, the option of revising it or even discarding it. Without a plan, the tendency is to settle for anything that looks good at the moment. Unfortunately, this can lead to a waste of time and energy. It frequently results in unnecessary problems that have to be resolved.

. . . SEEKING A HEIGHTENED STATE OF SELF-AWARENESS.

Many of the searching questions that you will be posing to the facilitators are also relevant for you as a trainer: "Who am I?" "What is important to me?" "How did I come to hold these beliefs?" "How do others see me?" "What do I do that influences this perception?"

Enhancing your self-awareness helps you to be more honest, sincere and congruent. It puts you in touch with your expectations. It increases your awareness of times when you may feel disappointed and impatient. It helps you focus on your goals—outcomes and experiences—that will be rewarding to you.

Knowing more about yourself enables you to trust your own judgment more and gives you the extra confidence needed to be more patient with students or give them a gentle push. It reduces the times when you project your needs and values on others.

How do you go about acquiring more self-awareness? You may already be involved in some type of self-examination or self-renewal process. This may be a planned self-directed program. It may be through a class. Or perhaps you are attending workshops which emphasize personal growth and exploration. Regardless of how much you already know about yourself, working with young people in a peer facilitator program is an excellent opportunity to learn even more.

You will want to try new ideas as a trainer and facilitator. You, too, can be facilitated. By participating in the class activities, you not only model an openness and readiness to learn, but you will make personal discoveries. You will learn more about "what makes you tick." Avoid being "super counselor" or "super trainer" —aloof from it all or above participating with the facilitators. Get involved with the learning process. Participate in some, if not most, of the activities. Share some of yourself with the students. Take a few risks. Disclose your ideas and feelings that are relevant and leave room for people to disagree with your point of view. Model the role of a helping person.

...IS COMMITTED TO THE PROGRAM AND ITS PHILOSOPHY.

You may be well-organized, knowledgeable and have an excellent understanding of yourself and others. Yet, without a personal commitment to the program, you will not be genuine or congruent. Commitment generates enthusiasm and excitement. It serves to intensify what is taking place. It communicates interest and caring. It is probably the most important ingredient for success.

Commitment makes the difficult days bearable and the successful ones sweeter. It is a special quality that must come from within you. Those facilitators who experience a trainer who is committed to helping them learn to be effective will, undoubtedly, have a more positve outlook and approach to their work.

WHAT BEGINNING TRAINERS HAVE SAID

"I'm excited about the concept. . . feeling motivated and can see its usefullness. I definitely want to initiate this concept in my school."

"I relearned that peers exert great influence on each other and that, with their help, I can reach more students than ever before."

"This is one of the most exciting developments in education today and I would like to tell more people about it!"

"I learned that when you think you are butting your head against a brick wall of indifference, there may be another way to make a dent—through peer facilitators."

"I learned that peer facilitators can help me make better use of my time."

"The skills that we teach peer facilitators are pertinent to all people in every walk of life. If we can model and practice good communication skills with others, then the world is going to be a better place."

"How can we say that kids are well-educated in our schools if we neglect one of the most important aspects of learning to live in our society—relationships and communication skills?"

"This stuff really works!"

"With guided training, peers can do much more than we expected and they become more involved in what we are trying to have them learn about themselves and others."

"I was experiencing 'counselor burnout' before I got involved with the peer facilitator program. Now, I find myself more motivated and have experienced some professional renewal. Most important, I'm closer to the students (students in general) than I've ever been before."

"Through teaching the students to be effective facilitators, I've sharpened my own skills in counseling. And, it's opened up some new ways of counseling students that I hadn't been willing to try before."

"The program at our school has brought me a lot of positive strokes because it has been so popular and things have gone so well. God knows that all of us counselors need a few more positive strokes."

"I began with a lot of skepticism and doubt. Well, I guess you'd have to say that I was defensive and worried whether it would cause me more problems than anything else. But, I'm really glad that I started and I plan to do even more next year!"

"It's one of the most rewarding things I've ever done in my work as a counselor. It's given me some very gratifying personal experiences that I'll cherish for a long time."

IN CONCLUSION . . .

You will find both your personal and profesional lives changing in some very positive and exciting ways as a result of your experiences as a trainer of peer facilitators. You may even want to keep you own *Notes to Myself* journal.

"I expect to pass through this world but once. Any good thing, therefore, that I can do or any kindness I can show to any fellow human being. . .LET ME DO IT NOW. . . .

SELECTED REFERENCES FOR TRAINERS

Canfield, J., & Wells, H. *100 Ways to Enhance Self-concept in the Classroom.* Englewood Cliffs, NJ: Prentice-Hall, 1976.

Daane, C. *The Vocational Exploration Group (VEG).* Tempe, AZ: Studies for Urban Man, l972.

Dinkmeyer, D. *DUSO (Developing Understanding of Self and Others).* Circle Pines, MN: American Guidance Service, 1970.

Gray, H.D., & Tindall, J.A. *Peer Counseling.* Muncie, IN: Accelerated Development, Inc., 1978.

Gray, H.D., & Tindall, J.A. *Peer Power.* Muncie, IN: Accelerated Development, Inc., 1978.

Howe, L. *Personalizing Education: Values Clarification and Beyond.* New York: NY: Harto., 1975.

Johnson, D. *Reaching Out.* Englewood Cliffs, NJ: Prentice Hall, 1972.

Myrick, R.D., & Erney, T. *Caring and Sharing: Becoming a Peer Facilitator.* Minneapolis, MN: Educational Media Corporation, 1978.

Myrick, R.D., Erney, T., & Sorenson, D. *Peer Facilitators: Youth Helping Youth* (27-minute 16 mm color film). Minneapolis, MN: Educational Media Corporation, 1976.

Myrick, R.D., & Sorenson, D. *Leading Group Discussions* (27-minute 16mm color film). Minneapolis, MN: Educational Media Corporation, 1978.

Palomares, U. *Human Development Program (Magic Circle).* La Mesa, CA: Human Development Training Institute, 1970.

Pfeiffer, W., & Jones, J. *A Handbook of Structured Experiences for Human Relations Trainers, Vols. I, II, III, IV and V.* Iowa City, IA: University Press, 1972.

Samuels, D., & Samuels, M. *The Complete Handbook of Peer Counseling.* Miami, FL: Fiesta Publishing Corp., 1975.

Simon, S., Howe, L., & Kirschenbaum, H. *Values Clarification: A Handbook of Practical Strategies for Teachers and Students.* New York, NY: Hart Publishing Co., 1972.

Special Issue: "Peer Facilitators," *Elementary School Guidance and Counseling Journal,.* 1976, *11* (1).

Wittmer, J., & Myrick, R.D. *Facilitative Teaching.* Minneapolis, MN: Educational Media Corporation, 1980.

BIBLIOGRAPHY

Allen, D.A. Underachievement is many-sided. *Personnel and Guidance Journal,* 1971, *49,* 529-532.

Allen, E.E. Paraprofessionals in a large-scale university program. *Personnel and Guidance Journal,* l974, *53,* 276-280.

Alwine, G. If you need love come to us; an overview of a peer counseling program in a senior high school. *Journal of School Health,* 1974, *44,* 463-464.

Anderson, R. Peer facilitation: history and issues. *Elementary School Guidance and Counseling,* 1976, *11* (1), 27-35.

Anderson, R.D., & Thompson, A.R. Mutually aided learning: An evaluation; high school students teach elementary science. *Journal of Research Science in Teaching,* 1971, *8,* 297-305.

Andrews, W.R. Behavioral and client-centered counseling of high school underachievers. *Journal of Counseling Psychology,* 1971, *18,* 93-96.

Armstrong, J.C. Perceived intimate friendship as a quasi-therapeutic agent. *Journal of Counseling Psychology,* 1969, *16,* 137-141.

Attwell, A.A. Some factors that contribute to underachievement in school: A suggested remedy. *Elementary School Guidance and Counseling,* 1968, *3,* 98-103.

Bakan, R. Academic performance and self-concept as a function of achievement-variability. *Journal of Educational Measurement,* 1971, *8,* 317-319.

Baker, V.K. Big friend: A tutorial program. *Educational Leadership,* 1973, *30,* 733-735.

Baldwin, B.A., & Wilson, R.R. An effective program with peer group counselors. *Tennessee Education,* 1973, *3* (3), 26-27.

Barcai, A., Unbarger, C., Pierce, T.W., & Chamberlain, P. Comparison of three group approaches to underachieving children. *American Journal of Orthopsychiatry,* 1973, *43,* 133-141.

Barclay, J.R. Effecting behavior change in the elementary classroom: An exploratory study. *Journal of Counseling Psychology,* 1967, *14,* 240-247.

Bates, M. A test of group counseling. *Personnel and Guidance Journal,* 1968, *46,* 749-753.

Baymur, F.B., & Patterson, C.H. A comparison of three methods of assisting underachieving high school students. *Journal of Counseling Psychology,* 1960, *7,* 83-90.

Bednar, R.L., & Weinberg, S.L. Ingredients of successful treatment programs for underachievers. *Journal of Counseling Psychology,* 1970, *17,* 1-7.

Bell, C. Personal correspondence, 1978.

Benson, R.L., & Blocher, D.H. Evaluation of developmental counseling with groups of low achievers in a high school setting. *School Counselor*, 1967, *14*, 215-220.

Biasco, F. The effects of individual counseling, multiple counseling, and teacher guidance upon the sociometric status of children enrolled in grades four, five, and six. *Dissertation Abstracts*, 1966, *27*, 223.

Blaker, H.E., Schmidt, M., & Jensen, W. Counselor-aides in guidance programs. *School Counselor*, 1971, *18*, 382-386.

Bloom, S. *Peer and cross-age tutoring in the schools*. Washington, D.C.: The National Institute of Education, 1976.

Bosdell, B.J., & Teigland, J.T. Problems discussed by underachievers in different treatment groups. *School Counselor*, 1965, *12*, 222-227.

Brach, A.M. Reaching young teens through group counseling. In Driver, H.I., *Counseling and Learning Through Small-Group Discussion*. Madison, WI: Monona Publications, 1958, 297-300.

Bramer, M. Who can be a helper? *Personnel and Guidance Journal*, 1977, *55*, 303-308.

Brandenbrug, J.B. Peer counseling for sex related concerns: A case study of a health service in a college medical setting. *Journal of the American College of Health Association*, 1976, *24* (5), 294-300.

Brown, W.F. Student-to-student counseling for academic adjustment. *Personnel and Guidance Journal*, 1965, *43*, 811-817.

Brown, W.F. *Student-to-student counseling*. Austin, TX: University of Texas Press, 1972.

Brown, W.F., Wehe, N.O., Zunker, V.G., & Haslam, W.L. Effectiveness of student-to-student counseling on the academic adjustment of potential college dropouts. *Journal of Educational Psychology*, 1971, *4*, 285-289.

Bry, B.H. A pilot course for the training of peer counselors for educationally disadvantaged students. *Teaching of Psychology*, 1975, *2*, 51-55.

Buck, M.R. Peer counseling. *School and Community*, 1977, *63*, 12.

Caditz, R. Using student tutors in high school mathematics; weak students profit from volunteer assistance. *Chicago School Journal*, 1963, *44*, 323-325.

Caplan, S.W. The effect of group counseling on junior high school boys' concepts of themselves in school. *Journal of Counseling Psychology*, 1957, *4*, 124-128.

Capone, T., McLaughlin, J.H., & Smith, F. Peer group leadership program in drug abuse prevention. *Journal of Drug Education*, 1973, *3* (3), 201-246.

Carkhuff, R.R. Training in the counseling and therapeutic practices: Requiem or reveille? *Journal of Counseling Psychology*, 1966, *13*, 364.

Carkhuff, R.R. Differential functioning of lay and professional helpers. *Journal of Counseling Psychology*, 1968, *15*, 117-126.

Carkhuff, R.R., & Griffin, A.H. Selection and training of a human relations specialist. *Journal of Counseling Psychology*, 1970, *17*, 443-450.

Carkhuff, R.R., & Truax, C.B. Training in counseling and psychotherapy: An evaluation of an integrated didactic and experiential approach. *Journal of Counseling Psychology*, 1965, *29*, 333-336.

Christine, R.O. Pupil-pupil teaching and learning team. *Education*, 1971, *91*, 258-260.

Cicirelli, V.G. Effect of sibling relationship on concept learning of young children taught by child-teachers. *Childhood Development*, 1972, *43*, 282-287.

Clack, R.J. Give a damn: A small group program for new students. *Journal of College Student Personnel*, 1975, *16*, 161.

Cloward, R.D. Studies in tutoring. *Journal of Experimental Education*, 1967, *36*, 14-25.

Collins, J.E.A. A comparative guidance study: Group counseling methods with selected underachieving ninth grade students. *Disseration Abstracts*, 1964, *25*, 3389.

Cooker, P.G., & Cheria, P.J. Effects of communication skill training on high school students' ability to function as peer group facilitators. *Journal of Counseling Psychology*, 1976, *23* (5), 464-467.

Coopersmith, S. *The Antecedents of Self-esteem.* San Francisco, CA: W. H. Freeman & Co., 1967.

Cote, T.J. Counselors' most logical helper. *American Vocational Journal*, 1968, *43* (1), 11-14.

Cowan, E.L., Dorr, D.A., Sandler, I.N., & McWilliams, D. Utilizations of a nonprofessional child-aide school mental health program. *Journal of School Psychology*, 1971, *9*, 131-136.

Cowan, W., W., Leibowitz, E., & Leibowitz, G. Utilization of retired people as mental health aides with children. *American Journal of Orthopsychiatry*, 1968, *38*, 900-909.

Criscuolo, N.P. Training tutors effectively. *Reading Teacher,* 1971, *25*, 157-159.

Crow, M.L. A comparison of three group counseling techniques with sixth graders. *Elementary School Guidance and Counseling*, 1971, *6*, 37-42.

Crutchfield, R.S. Social psychology and group processes. *Annual Review of Psychology,* 1954, 171.

Dahlem, G. Heterogeneous age group programs: A new area for counselors. *Elementary School Guidance and Counseling*, 1969, *4*, 154-155.

Dana, R.H. Crisis intervention by peers. *Journal of College Student Personnel*, 1974, *12* (2), 58-60.

Dawson, R.W. Personality and peer counselors: An Australian study. *Personnel and Guidance Journal*, 1973, *52* (1), 46-49.

Delworth, U. Training student volunteers. *Personnel and Guidance Journal*, 1974, *53*, 57-61.

Diedrich, R.C., & Jackson, P.W. Satisfied and dissatisfied students. *Personnel and Guidance Journal*, 1969, *47*, 641-649.

Dil, N., & Gotts, E.E. Improvement of arithmetic self-concept through combined positive reinforcement, peer interaction, and sequential curriculum. *Journal of School Psychology*, 1971, *9*, 462-472.

Dinkmeyer, D., & Caldwell, C. *Developmental Counseling and Guidance: A Comprehensive School Approach*. New York, NY: McGraw-Hill, 1970.

Dorosin, D. A peer counselor training program rationale, curriculum and evaluation: An initial report. *Journal of the American College Health Association*, 1977, *25* (4), 259-262.

Driver, H.I. *Multiple Counseling: A Small Group Discussion Method for Personal Growth*. Madison, WI: Monona Publications, 1954.

Duncan, J.A. Ethical considerations in peer group work. *Elementary School Guidance and Counseling*, 1976, *11* (1), 53-58.

Dyer, W.W., Vriend, J., & Murphy, P.A. Peer group counseling: A total school approach. *Momentum*, 1975, *6*, 8-15.

Edwards, S.S. Student helpers: Multilevel facilitation program. *Elementary School Guidance and Counseling*, 1976, *11* (1), 53-58.

Egan, G. *Encounter: Group Process for Interpersonal Growth*. Belmont, CA: Brooks/Cole Publishing Co., 1970.

Ehlert, R. Kid counselors. *School Counselor*, 1975, *22*, 260-262.

Elliot, A. Student tutoring benefits everyone. *Phi Delta Kappan*, 1973, *54*, 535-538.

Elliott, C.D. Personality factors and scholastic attainment. *British Journal of Educational Psychology*, 1972, *42*, 23-32.

Entwistle, N.J. Personality and academic attainment. *British Journal of Educational Psychology*, 1972, *42*, 137-151.

Erickson, M.R., & Cromack, T. Evaluating a tutoring program. *Journal of Experimental Education*, 1972, *41*, 27-31.

Ettkin, L., & Snyder, L. A model for peer group counseling based on role-playing. *School Counselor*, 1972, *19*, 215-218.

Fink, M.B. Self-concept as it relates to academic underachievement. *California Journal of Educational Research*, 1962, *13*, 57-62.

Fleming, J.C. Pupil tutors and tutees learn together. *Today's Education*, 1969, *58*, 22-24.

Frager, S., & Stein, C . Learning by teaching. *The Reading Teacher,* 1970, 403-405.

Frank, M. Peer group counseling: A challenge to grow. *School Counselor*, 1974, *2*, 267-272.

Fredicine, A.J., & Kramer, C.R. SIA: Students in action. *School Counselor*, 1971, *19*, 133-135.

Gartner, A., Kohler, M., & Reismann, F. Every child a teacher. *Childhood Education*, 1971, *48*, 12-16.

Gartner, A., Kohler, M., & Reismann, F. *Children teach children: Learning by teaching.* New York, NY: Harper and Row, 1971.

Gazda, G.M., & Larsen, M.J. A comprehensive appraisal of group and multiple counseling research. *Journal of Research and Development in Education,* 1968, *1*, 57-132.

Geiser, R.L. Some of our worst students teach! Report on a unique tutoring program. *Catholic School Journal*, 1969, *69*, 18-20.

Gelatt, H.B. School guidance programs. *Review of Educational Research*, 1969, *39*, 141-153.

Gellen, M.I. Nonacademic tutoring: An exploratory experience. *School Counselor*, 1972, *19*, 279-284.

Giles, J.R. Positive peer culture in the public school system. *NASSP Bulletin*, 1975, *59*, 22-28.

Glick, O. Person-group relationships and the effect of group properties on academic achievement in the elementary school classroom. *Psychology in the Schools*, 1969, *6*, 197-203.

Gold, M. Power in the classroom. *Sociometry*, 1958, *21*,(1).

Golin, N., & Safferstone, M. *Peer Group Counseling: A Manual for Trainers*. Miami, FL: Dade County Public Schools, 1971.

Gray, H.D., & Tindall, J. *Peer Counseling: An In-depth Look at Training Peer Helpers*. Muncie, IN: Accelerated Development, Inc., 1978.

Gray, H.D., & Tindall, J. *Peer Power: Becoming an Effective Peer Helper*. Muncie, IN: Accelerated Development, Inc., 1978.

Gruver, G. College students as therapeutic agents. *Psychological Bulletin*, 1971, *76* (2), 111-127.

Guerney, B., & Flumen, A. Teachers as psychotherapeutic agents for withdrawn children. *Journal of School Psychology*, 1970, *8*, 107-112.

Gumaer, J. Peer-facilitated groups. *Elementary School Guidance and Counseling*, 1973, *8*, 4-11.

Gumaer, J. Training peer facilitators. *Elementary School Guidance and Counseling,* 1976, *11*(1), 27-35.

Gutsch, K.V., Spinks, S.L., & Aitken, J.R. Counselor aides in action: Hattiesburg public schools, Mississippi. *Counselor Education and Supervision*, 1969, *9* (2), 61-63.

Hamburg, B.A., & Varenhorst, B.B. Peer counseling in the secondary schools: A community health project for youth. *American Journal of Orthopsychiatry*, 1972, *42*, 566-581.

Hansen, J.C., Niland, T.M., & Zani, L.P. Model reinforcement in group counseling with elementary school children. *Personnel and Guidance Journal,* 1969, *47*, 741-744.

Harris, M.M. Learning by tutoring others. *Today's Education*, 1971, *60*, 48-49.

Hartup, W.W., & Coates, B. Imitation of a peer as a function of reinforcement from the peer group and rewardingness of the model, *Childhood Development*, 1967, *38*, 1003-1016.

Hassinger, J., & Via, M. How much does a tutor learn through teaching reading? *Secondary Education,* 1969, *44*, 42-44.

Hawkins, T.E. Utilizing the services of the academically talented students. *Journal of Negro Education*, 1965, *34*, 93-95.

Hebeisen, A. *Peer Program for Youth* Minneapolis, MN: Augsburg Publishing House, 1973.

Heller, B., & Gurney, D. Involving parents in group counseling with junior high underachievers. *School Counselor*, 1968, *15*, 394-397.

Hewer, V.H. Group counseling. *Vocational Guidance Quarterly*, 1968, *15* (3), 250-257.

Hoffman,L.R. Peers as group counseling models. *Elementary School Guidance and Counseling,* 1976, *11* (1), 37-44.

Holzberg, J., Gerwirtz, H., & Ebner, E. Changes in self-acceptance and moral judgments in college students as a function of companionship with hospitalized patients. *Journal of Consulting Psychology*, 1964, *28*, 299-303.

Hosford, R.E., & Briskin, A.S. Changes through counseling. *Review of Educational Research*, 1969, *39*, 189-207.

Hummel, R., & Sprinthall, N. Underachievement related to interests, attitudes and values. *Personnel and Guidance Journal,* 1965, *44*, 388-395.

Jacobs, E. Peer helpers: An easy way to get started. *Elementary School Guidance and Counseling*, 1976, *11* (1), 68-71.

Kagan, J., & Moss, H. *Birth to Maturity*. New York, NY: Wiley, 1962.

Keelin, P.W. Training adolescents to collect behavioral data in the elementary school classroom. *Elementary School Guidance and Counseling*, 1975, *10*, 63-66.

Kelly, R., & Kirby, J. Utilizing peer helper influences in group counseling. *Elementary School Journal*, 1971, *6*, 70-75.

Kern, R., & Kriby, J.H. Utilizing peer helper influence in group counseling. *Elementary School Guidance and Counseling*, 1971, *6*, 70-75.

Khan, S.B. Affective correlates of academic achievement. *Journal of Educational Psychology*, 1969, *60*, 216-221.

Kinnick, B.C., & Shannon, J.T. The effect of counseling on peer group acceptance of socially rejected students. *School Counselor*, 1965, *12*, 162-166.

Kinnick, B.C. Group discussions and group counseling applied to student problem solving. *School Counselor*, 1968, *15*, 350-356.

Knapp, R.H., & Holzberg, J.D. Characteristics of college students volunteering for service to mental patients. *Journal of Consulting Psychology*, 1964, *28*, 82-85.

Koeppe, R.P., & Brancroft, J. Elementary and secondary school programs. *Review of Educational Research*, 1966, *36*, 219-232.

Lahaderne, H.M., & Jackson, P.W. Withdrawal in the classroom: A note on some educational correlates of social desirability among school children. *Journal of Educational Psychology*, 1970, *61*, 97-101.

Landrum, J.W., & Martin, M.D. When students teach others: One-to-one project, Los Angeles County Schools. *Educational Leadership*, 1970, *27*, 446-448.

Lane, P., Pollack, C., & Sher, N. Remotivation of disruptive adolescents. *Journal of Reading*, 1972, *15*, 351-354.

Lawrence, D. Counseling of retarded readers by nonprofessionals. *Educational Research*, 1972, *15*, 48-51.

Leibowitz, A., & Rhodes, D.J. Adolescent peer counseling. *School Counselor*, 1974, *21*, 280-283.

Leventhal, A.M. Peer counseling on the university campus. *Journal of College Student Personnel*, 1976, *17* (6), 504-508.

Lewis, S.O. Black counselor educators use peer counseling. *Journal of Non-White Concerns in Personnel and Guidance*, 1976, *5* (1), 6-13.

Lilly, M.S. Improving social acceptance of low sociometric status, low achieving students. *Exceptional Children*, 1971, *37*, 341-347.

Lippitt, P., & Lippitt, R. Peer culture as a learning environment. *Childhood Education*, 1970, *47* (3), 135-138.

Lippitt, R., & Lippitt, P. Cross-age helpers. *Education Digest*, 1968, *33*, 23-25.

Lippitt, P., & Lohman, J.E. Cross-age relationships: An educational resource. *Children*, 1965, *12*, 113-117.

Lobitz, W.C. Maximizing the high school counselor's effectiveness: The use of senior tutors. *School Counselor*, 1970, *18*, 127-129.

Lorish, Robert. *Teaching Counseling Skills to Disadvantaged Young Adults*. Unpublished Doctoral Dissertation, Boston University, 1974.

Lundberg, D.L.V. Some evaluations of tutoring by peers. *Journal of Secondary Education*, 1968, *48*, 99-103.

Lutker, C. Academic workshop: Use of paraprofessional leaders and behavior change goals for students on academic probation. *Journal of College Student Personnel*, 1975, *16*, 162-163.

Mackie, Peter. *Teaching Counseling Skills to Low Achieving High School Students*. Unpublished Doctoral Dissertation, Boston University, 1974.

Maher, C. Achieving with the underachiever. *Catholic School Journal*, 1969, *69*, 28-30.

Mahler, C.A. *Group counseling in the schools*. Boston, MA: Houghton Mifflin, 1969.

Mayer, G.R., Kranzler, G.D., & Matthes, W.A. Elementary school counseling and peer relations. *Personnel and Guidance Journal*, 1967, *46*, 360-365.

McCann, G.G. Peer counseling: An approach to psychological education. *Elementary School Guidance and Counseling*, 1975, *9*, 180-187.

McCarthy, B.W. Growth and development of a university companion program. *Journal of Counseling Psychology*, 1975, *22* (1), 66-69.

McCleary, E. Report of results of tutorial reading program. *Reading Teacher*, 1971, *24*, 556-560.

McCowan, R.J. The effect of "brief contact" interviews with low-ability, low-achieving students. *School Counselor*, 1968, *15*, 386-389.

McLaurin, R., & Harrington, J. High school instructional peer-counseling program. *Personnel and Guidance Journal*, 1977, *55*, 262-265.

McWhorter, K.T., & Levy, J. Influence of a tutorial program upon tutors. *Journal of Reading*, 1971, *14*, 221-224.

McWilliams, S.A., & Finkely, N.J. High school students as mental health aides in the elementary school setting. *Journal of Consulting and Clinical Psychology,* 1974, *42*, 244-250.

Miller, T. Peer counseling: A model for the selection and training of students to help students. *Counseling and Values*, 1973, *17* (3), 190-193.

Mosher, Ralph L. Funny things happen on the way to curriculum development. In Peters, H., & Aubrey, R. (Eds.) *Guidance: Strategies and Techniques*, Denver, CO: Love Publishing, 1975.

Mosher, Ralph, L., & Sprinthall, N.A. Psychological education: A means to promote personal development during adolescence. In Purpel, D.E., & Belanger, M. (Eds.) *Curriculum and the Cultural Revolution*, Berkeley, CA: McCutchan Publishing Corporation, 1972.

Mosher, R.L., & Sullivan, P. A curriculum in moral education for adolescents. In *Challenge in Educational Administration*, Edmonton, Alberta: Department of Educational Administration, University of Alberta, 1974.

Murphy, C. Peer teaching at Hofstra. *Change*, 1975, *7* (4), 22-24.

Murray, J. The comparative effectiveness of student-to-student and faculty advising programs. *Journal of College Student Personnel*, 1972, *13*, 47-51.

Myrick, R.D., Moni, L., & Simonis, S. The counselor's workshop: Learning centers— an approach to developmental guidance. *Elementary School Guidance and Counseling*, 1973, *8*, 58-63.

Nelson, G. High school students teach science in elementary grades. *American Biology Teacher*, 1972, *34*, 332-337.

Ney, L.A. A multiple counseling project for underachieving sixth graders. In Driver, H.I., *Counseling and Learning Through Small-group Discussion*. Madison, WI: Monona Publications, 1958, 291-293.

Niedermeyer, F.C., & Ellis, P. Remedial reading instruction by trained pupil tutors. *Elementary School Journal*, 1971, *71*, 400-405.

Norris, R.E., & Wantland, P.J. Big brothers and sisters assist readers. *School and Community*, 1972, *58*, 8+.

Paolitto, D. *Role Taking Opportunities for Early Adolescents: A Program in Moral Education*. Unpublished Doctoral Dissertation, Boston University, 1975.

Payne, D.A. *The Specification and Measurement of Learning Outcomes*. Waltham, MA: Blaisdell Publishg Co., 1968.

Perkins, H.V. Clarifying feelings through peer interaction. *Childhood Education*, 1969, *45*, 379-380.

Petrillo, R. Rap room: Self help at school. *Social Policy*, 1976, *7* (2), 54-58.

Porter, E.J. Project promise: Recruiting high school students for teaching in city schools. *Elementary English*, 1971, *48*, 336-340.

Poser, E.G. The effects of therapist's training on group therapeutic outcome. *Journal of Counseling Psychology*, 1966, *30*, 283-289.

Powell, O.B. The student who assumes counseling responsibilities. In Hardee, M.D. (Ed.) *The Faculty in College Counseling*. New York, NY: McGraw-Hill, 1959.

Pyle, K.R. Developing a teen peer facilitator program. *School Counselor*, 1977, *24* (4), 278-281.

Pyle, K.R., & Snyder, F.A. Students as paraprofessional counselors at community colleges. *Journal of College Student Personnel*, 1971, *12*, 259-262.

Ramirez, J.V. Effects of tutorial experiences on the problemsolving behavior of sixth-graders. *California Journal of Educational Research*, 1971, *22*, 80-90.

Rashbaum-Selig, M. Student patrols help a disruptive child. *Elementary School Guidance and Counseling*, 1976, *11* (1), 47-51.

Reynolds, C. Buddy system improves attendance. *Elementary School Guidance and Counseling*, 1977, *11* (1), 305-306.

Riessman, F., & Gartner, A. Paraprofessionals; the effect on children's learning. *Urban Review*, 1969, *4*, 21-22.

Rogers, C. Can schools grow persons? *Educational Leadership*, 1971, 217.

Rosenthal, R., & Jacobsen, L. *Pygmalion in the Classroom: Teacher Expectation and Pupil's Intellectual Development*. New York, NY: Holt, Rinehart & Winston, 1968.

Rossi, T.P. Help: Students teach students. *Reading Improvement*, 1969, *6*, 47-49.

Rudow, E.H. Paraprofessional in a drug education program. *Personnel and Guidance Journal*, 1974, *53*, 294-297.

Ryan, M.K., & Varenhorst, B.B. Middle/junior high school counselors' corner. *Elementary School Guidance and Counseling Journal*, 1973, *8* (1), 54-57.

Samuels, D., & Samuels, M. *The Complete Handbook of Peer Counseling*. Miami, FL: Fiesta Publishing Corp., 1975.

Samuels, D. Peer counseling: An ongoing guidance curriculum. *NASSP Bulletin*, 1977, *61* (410), 43-49.

Schmidt, W.E., & Tyler, V.O. The "pinpointing effect" vs. the "diffusion effect" of peer influence. *Psychology in the School*, 1975, *12* (4), 484-494.

Schmitt, L.C., & Furniss, L.E. An elementary adjunct: High school helpers. *Personnel and Guidance Journal*, 1975, *53* (10), 778-781.
Schweisheimer, W., & Walberg, H.J. A peer counseling experiment: High school students as small group leaders. *Journal of Counseling Psychology*, 1976, *17* (3), 398-400.

Scott, S.H., & Warner, R.W. Peer Counseling. *Personnel and Guidance Journal*, 1974, *53*, 228-231.

Seeman, J. Counseling children in groups. *School Counselor*, 1963, *8* (2), 343-349.

Shainauskas, J. High school seniors as counselor aides. *School Counselor*, 1975, *22*, 369-370.

Shapiro, J.G., & Voog, T. Effect of the inherently helpful person on student academic achievement. *Journal of Counseling Psychology* 1969, *16*, 505-509.

Shaver, J.P., & Nuhn, D. Effectiveness of tutoring underachievers in reading and writing. *Journal of Educational Research*, 1971, *65*, 107-112.

Shaw, J.S. Cross-age tutoring: How to make it work. *Nations Schools*, 1973, *91*, 43-46.

Simpson, L.A., Pate, R.H., & Burks, H.M. New approach: Group counseling with trained subprofessionals. *Journal of College Placement*, 1973, *33*, 41-43.

Skovholt, T. The client as helper: A means to promote psychological growth. *The Counseling Psychologist*, 1974, *4* (3), 58-64.

Smart, R.G., Bennett, C. & Fejer, D. A controlled study of the peer group approach to drug education. *Journal of Drug Education*, 1976, *6* (4), 305-311.

Snadowsky, A., & Myer, D. Meeting a higher education goal through a student volunteer counseling program. *Improving College and University Teaching*, 1975, *23*, 182-183.

Snapp, M. Study of individualized instruction by using elementary school children as tutors. *Journal of School Psychology*, 1972, *10*, 1-8.

Solomon, C. Student to student counseling. *Change*, 1974, *6* (8), 48-50.

Southworth, R.S. A study of the effects of short-term group counseling on underachieving sixth grade students. *Dissertation Abstracts*, 1966, *27*, 1272-1273-A.

Spiegel, S.B. College student's preferences for peer and professional counselors. *Vocational Guidance Quarterly*, 1976, *24*, 196-197.

Spivack, G., & Swift, M.S. *Devereaux-Elementary School Behavior Rating Manual*. Devon, PA: The Devereaux Foundation, 1967.

Sprinthall, N.A., & Erickson, V.L. Learning psychology by doing psychology: Guidance through the curriculum. *Personnel and Guidance Journal*, 1974, *52*, 396-405.

Stanley, S. *A Curriculum to Affect the Moral Atmosphere of the Family and the Moral Development of Adolescents.* Unpublished Doctoral Dissertation, Boston University, 1975.

Starlin, C. Peers and precision; first grade class. *Teaching Exceptional Children*, 1971, *3*, 129-132.

Steenland, R. Paraprofessionals in counseling centers. *Personnel and Guidance Journal*, 1973, *51*, 417-418.

Stein, A.H. Influence of social reinforcement on the achievement behavior of fourth-grade boys and girls. *Childhood Development*, 1969, *40*, 727-736.

Stewart, L., Dawson, D. & Byles, J. Using peer-group intervention with problem students in a secondary school. *Hospital and Community Psychiatry*, 1976, *27* (8), 572-574.

Stormer, G.E. Milieu group counseling in elementary school guidance. *Elementary School Guidance and Counseling*, 1967, *1*, 239-254.

Sue, S. Training of third world students to function as counselors. *Journal of Counseling Psychology*, 1973, *20*, 73-78.

Sullivan, P. *A Curriculum for Stimulating Moral Development in Adolescents.* Unpublished Doctoral Dissertation, Boston University, 1975.

Teahan, J.E. Parental attitudes and college success. *Journal of Educational Psychology*, 1963, *54*, 104-109.

Thelen, H.A. Tutoring by students. *Education Digest*, 1970, *35*, 17-20.

Thombs, M.R., & Muro, J.J. Group counseling and the sociometric status of second grade children. *Elementary School Guidance and Counseling*, 1973, *7*, 194-197.

Thoresen, C.E., & Hamilton, J.A. Peer social modeling in promoting career behaviors. *Vocational Guidance Quarterly*, 1972, *20* (3), 113-117.

Tiegland, J.J., Winkler, R.C., Munger, P.F., & Kranzler, G.D. Some concomitants of underachievement at the elementary school level. *Personnel and Guidance Journal*, 1966, *44*, 950-955.

Toffler, A. *Future Shock.* New York, NY: Random House, 1970.

Truax, C.B., & Lister, J.L. Effectiveness of counselors and counselor aides. *Journal of Counseling Psychology*, 1970, *17*, 331-334.

Tucker, S.J. Personality and status profiles of peer counselors and suicide attempters. *Journal of Counseling Psychology*, 1975, *22* (5), 423-429.

Turner, A.L., & Archer, J. Black peer counseling program. *College Student Personnel*, 1976, *17*, 155.

Vacc, N. The role of paraprofessional counselors in a university drug abuse program. *College Student Journal*, 1973, *7*(4), 41-46.

Vander Kolk, C.J. Paraprofessionals as psychotherapeutic agents with moderately disturbed children. *Psychology in the Schools*, 1973, *10*, 238-242.

Van Wagenen, R.C. Student tutors effective in high school business programs. *Business Education Forum*, 1969, *24*, 7-8.

Varenhorst, B.B. Peer counseling program. *Elementary School Guidance and Counseling*, 1973, *8*, 54-57.

Varenhorst, B.B., & Hamburg, B.A. *Peer Counselor Program and Curriculum.* Palo Alto, CA: Palo Alto Unified School District, 1971.

Varenhorst, B.B. Training adolescents as peer counselors. *Personnel and Guidance Journal*, 1974, *53* (4), 271-275.

Vassallo, W. Learning by tutoring. *American Education*, 1973, *9*, 25-28.

Vorrath, H. *Positive Peer Culture.* Lansing, MI: Michigan Center for Group Studies, 1972.

Vriend, T.J. High-performing inner-city adolescents assist low-performing peers in counseling groups. *Personnel and Guidance Journal*, 1969, *47*, 897-904. (a)

Vriend, T.J. The peer influence model in counseling. *Educational Technology*, 1969, *9*, 50-51. (b)

Walker, C. The use of high school and college students as therapists and researchers in a state mental hospital. *Psychotherapy: Theory, Research, and Practice*, 1967, *4* (4), 186-188.

Weise, R. Diary of a peer facilitator program. *Elementary School Guidance and Counseling*, 1976, *11* (1), 63-66.

Weitzman, D.L. Effect of tutoring on performance and motivation ratings in secondary school students. *California Journal of Educational Research*, 1965, *16*, 108-115.

West, J.H., & Ray, P.B. The helper therapy principle in relation to self concept change in commuter peer counselors. *Journal of College Student Personnel*, 1977, *18* (4), 301-305.

Westbrook, R.D., & Smith, J.B. Assisting black resident students at a predominately white institution: A paraprofessional approach. *Journal of College Student Personnel*, 1976, *17* (3), 205-209.

Winkler, R.C., Tiegland, J.J., Munger, P.F., & Kranzler, G.D. The effects of selected counseling and remedial techniques on underachieving elementary school students. *Journal of Counseling Psychology*, 1965, *53*, 778-781.

Winters, W.A., & Arent, R. The use of high school students to enrich an elementary guidance and counseling program. *Elementary School Guidance and Counseling*, 1969, *3*, 198-205.

Wittmer, J. The effects of counseling and tutoring on the attitudes and achievement of seventh grade underachievers. *School Counselor*, 1969, *16*, 287-290.

Wrenn, R.L., & Mencke, R. Students who counsel students. *Personnel and Guidance Journal*, 1972, *50*, 687-689.

Zapf, R.G. Rap shack: Using volunteer counselors. *Personnel and Guidance Journal*, 1973, *52*, 105-108.

Zax, M., Cowen, E., Izzo, L., Madonia,A., Merenda, J., & Trost, M. A teacher-aid program for preventing emotional disturbances in young school children. *Mental Hygiene*, 1966, *50*, 406-415.

Zunker, V.G. Students as paraprofessionals in four year colleges and universities. *Journal of College Student Personnel*, 1975, *16* (4), 282-286.

Zunker, V.G., & Brown, W.F. Comparative effectiveness of student and professional counselors. *Personnel and Guidance Journal*, 1966, *44*, 738-743.